MONOGRAPHIC JOURNALS OF THE NEAR EAST
SYRO-MESOPOTAMIAN STUDIES 5/2 (April 1993)
A publication of
IIMAS — The International Institutute for Mesopotamian Area Studies

SMS 5/2

FIVE TABLETS FROM THE SOUTHERN WING OF PALACE G — EBLA

Alfonso Archi

Malibu 1993
Undena Publications

The series *Monographic Journals of the Near East* includes medium size monographs, published independently of each other and without any periodical schedule. For convenience, they are grouped into volumes which are closed when a total of about 200 pages is reached. Individual titles are available on a standing order basis, which can be placed with the publisher for each of the various journals. —Beginning with 1991, the text portion of most monographs is available on disk in MS-DOS/ASCII format, within the series *Cybernetica Mesopotamica: Electronic Editions*, which is also distributed by Undena Publications.

The journal *Syro-Mesopotamian Studies* is devoted to the study of the civilizations which flourished in the area characterized by the use of Sumerian and Akkadian, from late prehistory to the end of the First Millennium B.C., providing an outlet for the publication of primary sources and a forum for the archaeological, linguistic and historical analysis of pertinent phenomena.

SMS 5/2. — The five tablets published here were discovered during the campaigns of 1982 and 1984 in the southern wing of Palace G. They represent the most recently discovered epigraphic finds from Ebla. The texts consist of accounts of goods under the control of the palace, deliveries of jars of wine, and deliveries of quantities of damp malt. As all of these tablets were recovered in the same general vicinity, it is suggested that the administrative bureau responsible for the handling of and accounting for wine and malt was located in this area. Of particular interest are the texts that recount the deliveries of wine and malt for they are typologically without parallel in the central archive. All five of these documents are datable to the last period of Ebla.

ISBN: 0-89003-277-7

Table of Contents

List of Plates

Text Copies

Photographs

List of Figures

Description

Five Tablets from the Southern Wing of Palace G - Ebla

Alfonso Archi

1. Introduction

The five administrative texts that are published here were found in the southern wing of Palace G of Ebla (fig. 1), at the foot of the slope of the Acropolis, during the campaigns of the years 1982 and 1984. Numbers 2 and 3 come from the floor of room L.3143. Number 1, whose contents are the same as number 2, comes from the adjacent room L.3462. Number 4, whose contents are the same as number 3, was found further east, on the floor of L.3474. Number 5 was discovered near wall M.3652, which delimits room L.3654, beside L.3474 (fig. 2).[1]

These tablets do not, therefore, constitute part of an archive. The fact that they were found in several rooms suggests that the bureau where the allotments of wine and malt were controlled, detailed lists of which are given in texts 3-5, was adjacent. The impressive summaries of goods possessed by the Palace recorded in documents 1 and 2 demonstrate, however, that the person who was in charge of coordinating the entire administration worked in those rooms.

The documents present typologies which differ from those in the texts preserved in the central archive (L.2769). Lists of deliveries of jars of wine (dug geštin), such as numbers 3 and 4, and of quantities of damp malt (GIŠ-a-mùnu), number 5, find no parallels there. Large sums relative to sheep or to fields and amounts of cereals are found in the central archive, but none of the texts there include total data of such diverse goods as those recorded in tablet 2. Also the recording of deliveries of foodstuffs in archive L.2712, published in *ARET* IX and forthcoming in X, and the long lists of quantities of cereals, each designated by the name of the place of production, which constitute part of the lot of tablets found in L.2764, have few parallels in the central archive.[2]

The new find confirms that the statements of accounts for the central archives were prepared in a different manner than those of the sectorial administrative offices. And as is exemplified by the wine production accounts, not all of the data flowed into the central archive. On the other hand, specific documents, such as instructions and general accounts

---

[1] I wish to thank James Platt for his editorial advice. The photos were provided by Maurizio Necci.

[2] For a description of the archives of Ebla, see Archi in K.R. Veenhof, *Cuneiform Archives and Libraries* (Leiden 1986) pp. 72-86; P. Matthiae, *ibid*, pp. 53-71.

(our nos. 1 and 2), could have been recorded for the purpose of being preserved in the administration's operative sectors.[3]

The five texts date to the last period of Ebla. The last of the viziers, Ibbi-Zikir, is mentioned in numbers 1-4, his son Dubuḫu-Ada in number 4, and his agent, Šema-Kura, in number 5. Like many of the small tablets in the central archive, these too are unbaked. Those from archive L.2712, in general pink in color with the exception of a few black ones, are all small in size, but are, in contrast, well baked. In some cases, however, the inner nucleus has turned to dust. This could indicate that originally the tablets of L.2712 were also unbaked, or that some of them were poorly baked, and that the heat of the fire that destroyed Palace G hardened the surface of some of them but without reaching the nucleus.

2. Totals of goods controlled by the Palace

Text No. 1: TM.82.G.267[4]
(Copy on Plate I and photographs on Plate IX)

			(1)
Obv.	I	1	1 *ma-ḫu-at* 6 *rí-pap* 1 *li* 4 *mi-at* 60 še *gú-bar*
			en[a)]
		3	*wa*[a)]
	II	1	*I-bí-zi-kir*
			(2)
			zé-*su-ma*
		3	en
			3 dumu-nita
		5	níg-gul:é
			(3)
			nu-zé
	III	1	nu-níg-gul:é
			(4)
			7 *rí-pap* 1 *li* GÁNA-ki
		3	lú en
			(uninscribed)

[3] It is possible to demonstrate that for section (5) of tablet no. 2 the scribe has made use of a detailed account concerning cattle, TM.75.G.10213, kept in the main archive; see below the commentary to that text.

[4] The tablet has been found in room L.3462, on the floor. It measures 54 × 59 mm.

			(5)
Rev.	I	1	šu-nígin! 9 *rí-pap* 2 *li* 7 ⌜*mi-at*⌝ ⌜udu⌝
			en
		3	*wa*
			I-bí-zi-kir
	II	1	1 *li* 4 *mi* 10 maḫ:gu$_4$
			1 *li* gu$_4$-tur
			(6)
		3	zé-*su-ma*
			en
		5	3 dumu-nita
			níg-gul:é
			(7)
	III	1	nu-zé-*su-ma*
			nu-níg-gul:é
			(8)
		3	en
			dub
			(9)
		5	iti *ir-mu*

a) Written on an erased case.

(1)

161,460 measures *gubar* of barley (under the jurisdiction) of the king and of Ibbi-Zikir.

(2)

Their (i.e. the king and Ibbi-Zikir)[5] withdrawal the king places at the disposal of (his) three sons.

(3)

(If) there is no withdrawal, (those goods) cannot be at their disposal.

---

[5] *-su-ma* (obv. II 2, rev. II 3, III 1) is the dual form of the suffixal personal pronoun, see P. Fronzaroli, *Festschrift. S. Segert*, *MAARAV* 5-6 (1990) p. 121.

(4)

71,000 measures GÁNA-ki of fields are (under the jurisdiction) of the king.

(5)

Grand total: 92,700 sheep (under the jurisdiction) of the king and of Ibbi-Zikir. 1,410 adult cattle and 1,000 calves.

(6)

Their (i.e. the king and Ibbi-Zikir) withdrawal the king places at the disposal of (his) three sons.

(7)

(If) there is no withdrawal, (those goods) cannot be at their disposal.

(8)

The king (has issued) the document.

(9)

IX month.

The document is comprised of two parallel sections: the disposition of a large quantity of barley and fields (obverse), and a large number of sheep (reverse), respectively, belonging to the king and his vizier Ibbi-Zikir. The accounting data: "161,460 measures of barley / 92,700 sheep of the king and Ibbi-Zikir," are followed in both cases by the same expression that is later repeated in a negative form, a turn of phrase that can be expected in a decree or in a letter, but which is extraneous to the accounting style:

zé-*su-ma*...níg-é-gul / nu-zé(-*su-ma*) nu-níg-é-gul

The unknown terminology and the generic reference to "three sons," 3 dumu-nita, to whom the formula refers, do not permit us to understand the purpose of the document, which certainly establishes certain privileges in favor of the "three sons," but does not take the usual form of a decree: *en-ma* en "Thus the king...." The omission of the personal names of these children and the lack of the year date here, as in so many other documents, are facts that contrast with the precision that the Palace's administration imposed on account keeping, accounting for every single unit of the goods it was responsible for. But the accounts were one thing and the administrative decrees were another. In the latter, motives were often omitted; the specification of benefits and the identification of the goods in question were summarized. A document, however, served as proof, and it was recorded for this reason. Even if the majority of the Eblaite documents are tersely formulated, the members of the Palace administration were, in any case, directly aware of the pertinent data.

The key to understanding the text is to determine the meaning of the terms zé and níg-gul:é (obv. II 2, 5 rev. II 3, 6; in the negative form, preceded by nu-, in obv. II 6, III 1, and rev. III 1-2). In the lexical lists zé is not glossed, while in list D there is níg-é-gul-gul (this text provides the proper order in which the signs have to be read) = *en-nu*, and in TM.75.G.1678 obv. V 6: níg-é-gul-gul, 7-8: níg-é-gul-gul-LUM = *ʾà-na-núm*. This word is the same as the Akkadian *enēnu* "to pray, ask for mercy," while *en-nu* has to be something like "gracious, gratuitous gift," in the administrative use "goods at someone's disposal."[6]

A meaning of this kind is confirmed by administrative practice. In *ARET* I 5, and only in this text among those published, níg-é-gul-gul qualifies certain deliveries of clothing. Section (54): 17+17 garments níg-é-gul-gul NP_1-NP_{17} lú muḫaldim-muḫaldim; section (78): 15+15 garments níg-é-gul-gul ḪÚB.KI; Section (79): 3+3 garments 3 nar-maḫ 23+23 garments níg-é-gul-gul nar-tur *Ma-rí*[ki]. On similar occasions, such as deliveries for "the singers of Mari" in *ARET* IV 1 (24)-(25); VIII 523 (37); 531 (49), the need is not felt for such a qualification, indicating that there was nothing particular distinctive about the delivery and that it was most probably something like a "free gift."

The term zé occurs rather rarely in the economic documents. For example, it is found in *ARET* VIII 533 (5): 1+1+1 garments PN zé *si-in* É×PAP; 540 (23): 2+2+2 garments NP_1 lú zé NP_2 lú NP_3. Keeping in mind that it is translated in Akkadian with *nasāḫu* "to remove, deduct, transfer (people)," (*CAD* N, 2, p. 1), zé should mean "withdrawal." Therefore, *ARET* VIII 533 records a "withdrawal" for a funeral ceremony, and VIII 540 a "withdrawal" for one person to be delivered to another person.[7]

In the prescript documents and those of the chancellery, zé is, instead, relatively frequent. The Treaty with Abarsal, II 194-204, reads: en *A-bar-sal₄*[ki] *in* kalam-*tim* udu è DU.DU *mu-ù* zé-*sù su-ma* nu-ì-na-sum ì-a-è "The king of Abarsal will let the sheep go out (to pasture) in (his) country, and the water (will be) his withdrawal (i.e. it will be under his jurisdiction to give water); if he does not give (it), he will break (the oath)."[8] Sometimes zé is linked to verbs that mean "receive" or "give," as in TM.76.G.234 obv. V 12-VI 3: 1 gín DILMUN bar_6:kù 2 níg-sagšu zíd šu-ba_4-ti *wa* zé x["he has received 1 shekel of silver 2 measures n. of flour, and the withdrawal.]..."; TM.76.G.190 obv. II 6-9: [x]-*ma* [ì-n]a-sum-*sù a-da-wa* lú zé-*sù*. Further, TM.76.G.87 obv. I 6-II 2: še-ba ir_{11}-ir_{11} še-mar-ḫúb lú zé sa_6 lú še-ba ì-na-sum "the rations for the hungry[9] serfs they will draw plentifully, they will give (them) the rations!"

Document number 1 decrees, therefore, that the "three sons" (obv. II 4, rev. II 5) could make use of the withdrawals effected by the king and his vizier Ibbi-Zikir from the goods that we can define as being under the Palace's jurisdiction. However, they could have access to those goods only through the king and the vizier, and not directly: "Their (i.e. the king and Ibbi-Zikir) withdrawal the king places at the disposal of (his) three sons. (If) there is no withdrawal, (those goods) cannot be at their disposal," (sections [2]-[3], [6]-[7]). We

---

[6] See K. Hecker, *BaE*, p. 212; in note 46 he refers also to the equivalence: ù-gul-gá-gá = *utnēnu* in an Akkadian list, see *CAD* E, p. 163a. Cfr. G. Conti, in P. Fronzaroli, *MisEb* 3, p. 70.

[7] Similarly in *ARET* VII 48 (3): 3 ma-na tar kù-bar_6 4 kù-sal tar kù-bar_6 zé-sù ... *Ib-u₉-mu-ud*; here 30 shekels have been "drawn" from Ibumud. Zé has another meaning in the compound in GIŠ-ša-zé; see the indices to *ARET* IX, X.

[8] Cfr. E. Sollberger, *SEb* 3 (1980), p. 138.

[9] For the interpretation of the gloss: še-mar-ḫúb = *ì-ma-zu-um*, Akk. *emēṣum* "to be hungry," see J. Krecher, *BaE*, p. 141.

do not know who the "three sons" are who are the beneficiaries of this decree. Obviously they had to be readily identifiable by members of the administration, but this cannot be seen from the administrative texts. Also in the delivery lists of sheep, partly for cult offerings, dated to Ebla's final period and therefore contemporary to this document, "king's sons" are mentioned, but they are enumerated in lists of eight or nine persons.[10] Since the beneficiaries of the instruction remain unknown, the meaning of the document as it pertains to administrative practice also remains unclear.

The fact that the king and the vizier are associated here in relation to such a large number of goods is an anomaly. In other documents, quantities of this kind are attributed only to the king or to the Palace, SA.ZA$_x$. The vizier is, instead, responsible for large "deliveries," mu-DU, to the Palace.[11] Here, it may have been intended that both the king and the vizier had access to those goods. Usually, they are found in association as recipients of a few goods, such as two girdles, *ARET* IV 6 (28); 7 (11); or two objects in gold, TM.75.G.1923 obv. XI 2-4; 2507 rev. II 6-8; 2508 obv. VII 38-40.[12]

Another anomaly is the syntactic relationship: en dub, in section (8). Normally, dub "tablet, document," is followed by a substantive whose function is that of a qualifying genitive, dub lugal: *ARET* VII 7 (7), 12 rev. III 1; dub GÁNA-ki šeš-mu PN: II 27 (14); dub dam-en: IX 52 (19); dub *ù-su-rí*: II 32 (18). The proposed translation: "The king (has issued) the document," is a good example of how much latitude texts of this kind leave to the imagination of their interpreters.

Text No. 2: TM.82.G.266[13]
(Copy on Plates II-III and photographs on Plates X-XI)

(1)

Obv. I 1 4 *ma-i-at* 2 *rí-pap* 1[+1$^?$] *li* GÁNA-ki
I-da-ne-ki-mu

(2)

3 6 ⌈*li*⌉ 6 *m*[*i*] GÁNA-ki
Du-b[*í-*]*ga*[*-lu*]

(3)

5 4 *m*[*a*]*-i-a*[*t*]
II 1 6 *rí-pap* 4 *li* še *gú-bar*
1 *rí-pap* 60 *gú-bar* sig$_{15}$
3 *I-da-ne-ki*[*-mu*]

(4)

---

[10] For example, in TM.75.G.1945 obv. VI 25-VII 7. Four of these texts have been published by G. Pettinato, *OA* 18 (1979), pp. 85-215.

[11] See for example *MEE* II 1 obv. IV 8-9, where the vizier is Ibrium, father of Ibbi-Zikir.

[12] See however TM.75.G.10191 obv. V 10-VI 13, here below in 5.2. sub *Kak-mi-um*^{ki}, where the king and Ibbi-Zikir receive vines and 90 vessels, dug, of wine from the city of Kakmium.

[13] The tablet was found on the floor of room L.3143. It measures 83 × 93 mm.

			[...]
		5	[...]
			[(..)]
			(5)
	III	1	9 *li* $2^{!}$+7[a] *mi-at* 41 gu$_4$
			3 *mi* 90 lá-1 ma-na bar$_6$:kù-[*s*]*ù*?
		3	[20+]5[b] ma-na šú+ša kù-gi
			níg-sa$_{10}$ (NÍNDA×ŠE.ZA)
	IV	1	7 *mi* 60 peš:áb lú edin
			6 *rí-pap* 4 *li* 5 *mi-at* 15 udu
		3	en
			(erased)
	V		(erased)
			(6)
Rev.[c]	I	1	7 *rí-pap* 3 *mi-at* GÁNA-ki
			Bù-ma-ù
			(7)
		3	1 *ma-ḫu-at* še *gú-bar*
			en
		5	(erased)
	II	1	(erased)
			(8)
			2 *ma-i-at* 2 *rí-pap* 1 *li* 5 *mi* 20 še *gú*<*-bar*>
		3	3 ugula ká
			lú *Si-si*^{ki}
		5	(uninscribed)
			(9)
	III	1	7 *mi-at* gu$_4$-maḫ
			Bù-ma-ù
		3	*in*[d]
			gi-li
		5	udu
			I-bí-zi-kir
			(10)
		7	5 *rí-pap* 4 *li* 2 *mi* udu
			en[a]
	IV	1	šu-du$_8$
			(11)
			1 *li* 5 *mi* ma-na kù-gi
		3	níg-sa$_{10}$ (NÍNDA×ŠE.ZA)
			ba-rúm
			(12)
		5	1 *li* ma-na bar$_6$:kù
			Ba-aš-dar

			(13)
		7	8 *mi* ma-na bar$_{6}$:kù
			še-SAG×ḪA-mul
		9	*Kam$_{4}$-lu-lu*^{ki}
			(14)
			8 *mi*
	V	1	ma-na bar$_{6}$:kù
			še-SAG×ḪA-mul
		3	*Ù-ti*
			(15)
			1 *li* 7 *mi* ma-na bar$_{6}$:kù
		5	nig-sa$_{10}$ (NÍNDA×ŠE.ZA$^{!}$)
			GIŠ-taškarin(TÚG)
		7	GIŠ-ir:nun
			(uninscribed)
Obv.	VI	1	lú *I-bí-zi-kir*
			(uninscribed space)

a) The number 9 is restored according to TM.75.G.10213 obv. IV 2. The first two units are poorly written, and were probably added later (see commentary).
b) Restoration according to TM.75.G.10213 rev. I 1.
c) Written from left to right.
d) Written in an erased case.

(1)
422,000 measures GÁNA-ki of field: Idanekimu.
(2)
6,600 measures GÁNA-ki of field: Dubigalu.
(3)
464,000 measures *gubar* of barley; 10,060 measures *gubar* of sig$_{15}$-cereal: Idanekimu.
(4)
[....]
(5)
9,941 cattle [who]se silver (i.e. value) is 389 minas; 25.20 minas of gold the value of 760 young cows[14] of the steppe,[15] 64,515 sheep: the king.

---

[14] peš:áb is attested in the lexical lists in the sequence: gu$_{4}$/peš:áb/amar, and without Eblaite equivalence. The five manuscripts of the unilingual List of Animals B (TM.75.G.10005+, 10025+, 4019+, 1947+, 2638+) have: ga-áb/áb/gar-ud-áb/ŠÀ×SAL-áb/amar-gaba-áb/peš-áb. Both áb-ŠÀ×SAL and áb-peš are attested in the economic texts, and áb-ŠÀ×SAL (in TM.75.G.2349 rev. VI 5 between gu$_{4}$-áb-UD.KEŠDA and amar-1-mu), has been explained as "pregnant cow" because in the bilingual list ŠÀ×SAL has the equivalence: *ʾà-ri-tum* "pregnant," Archi, *SEb* 7 (1984), p. 61 note 12. However, it is uncertain that áb-ŠÀ×SAL and áb-peš have different meanings in the Eblaite administrative texts (peš corresponds to Akkadian *libbu*). áb-peš is a "young cow" (A. Deimel, *ŠL* II.2, p. 631: "junge Kuh"), which is old enough to become pregnant, but not necessarily pregnant.

(6)

70,300 measures GÁNA-ki of field: Bumau.

(7)

100,000 measures *gubar* of barley: the king.

(8)

221,520 *gubar* of barley: the three overseers of the 'gate' (i.e. an administrative section) of the town of Sisi.[16]

(9)

700 heads of adult cattle: Bumau, in *custody*[17] (with) the sheep of Ibbi-Zikir.

(10)

54,200 sheep: the king has taken into possession.

(11)

1,500 minas of gold, value of (/for buying) *ba-rúm*.

(12)

1,000 minas of silver: Ba-Ašdar.

(13)

800 minas of silver, debt with interest: the town of Kamlulu.[18]

(14)

800 mana of silver, debt with interest: Uti.

(15)

1,700 minas of silver, value of boxwood and scented wood of *cedar*: belonging to Ibbi-Zikir.

The reading order of the two faces is from left to right, and both begin with the recording of the areas of fields and measures of barley. It is probable that the scribe began from the face that here is considered the obverse, and that for some reason he then cancelled the last case in column IV and all column V, deciding to begin again on the other side, from the left. Since there was not enough space for the last two words: lú *I-bí-zi-kir*, they were written in column VI of the obverse side, rather narrow because writing here had not been foreseen.

The very high quantities of goods on this tablet are attributed to some officials in addition to the king and vizier Ibbi-Zikir.

This is supported by the ritual TM.75.G.1939+ rev. VI 22-23, a reference pointed out to me by P. Fronzaroli, where 1 peš-áb nu-GIŠ-gál-"taka₄" "one not yet opened (i.e., not yet impregnated) young cow" is offered to the Sun deity. Sumerian gál-taka-a means "opened," and the Eblaite equivalent of GIŠ-gál-"taka₄" in the bilingual lists is *[b]a-da/du-um*, cfr. Akk. *petû*, a handle to open a door, see J. Krecher, *BaE*, p. 142; *ARET* IV, p. 297.

[15] The lexical lists have: edin = *za-lum* /ṣal-um/, *Ar. zaḥr, Akk. ṣēru* "steppe," cfr. Hecker, *BaE*, p. 216 note 68.

[16] Cfr. perhaps *Si-si-ù*[ki], *ARET* VIII 522 (4).

[17] For *gi-li* cfr. perhaps Akk. *kalû* "to detain, to keep in custody," and *ktlu*.

[18] Some workers dependent upon the Palace, like smiths and carpenters, resided in Kamlulu; see text no. 4 obv. V 3-4, 7-8.

Ba-aš-dar (section [12]: 1,000 minas of silver): the name is uncommon. It is therefore probable that this is the same as *Ba-^{d}Aš-dar* from the city of GudadaLUM, attested in *ARET* VIII 522 (12) ll. XII 4-13: 1+1 garments *Ì-lum-bal* maškim *I-bí-zi-kir* ḫi-mu-DU šeš *Ba-^{d}Aš-dar Kab-lu$_5$-ul^{ki} in Gú-da-da*-LUM^{ki}; (15): 1+1 garments *Mi-ga*-NI lú *Da-zi-ma-ad* níg-dingir-dingir-dingir-dingir en šeš *Ba-^{d}Aš-dar* šu-du$_8$; (16): 1+1 garments 1 dib 1 ma-na en *Gú-da-da*-LUM^{ki} šu-du$_8$ šeš *Ba-^{d}Aš-dar*.

Bù-ma-ù (section [9]): 700 head of adult cattle): it is doubtful that this person can be identified with *Bù-ma*-NI, a brother of Ibrium.[19]

Du-bí-ga-lu (section [2]: 6,600 GÁNA-ki): is a rather frequent name. A possible candidate is the Dubigalu associated with Irag-Damu in the lot of tablets from L.2752. In *ARET* VIII 541 (10) he is pa$_4$-šeš of Irag-damu, and in 527 (32), 529 (2) his maškim. See further, 533 (14): 2 dam *Ìr-ʾà-ag-da-mu Du-bí-ga-lu* šu-ba$_4$-ti; 522 (22): Idanikimu... en... Irag-Damu... Ibbi-Zikir... GurdaLUM... Dubigalu; 541 (45): en... *maliktum*... Irag-damu... Ibbi-Zikir... Ingar... Dubigalu.

I-da-ne-ki-mu (sections [1] and [3]: 422,000 GÁNA-ki, 464,000 *gubar* še, 10,060 *gubar* sig$_{15}$): is a "son of the king" of the first generation,[20] attested also in document number 3 in this lot of tablets.

Ù-ti (section [14]: 800 minas silver še-SAG×ḪA-mul): is a son of Ibrium.[21]

In total the following goods are listed: a) 498,900 measures of fields GÁNA-ki, which could mean about 17,601 hectares, more than 15 km^2; b) 795,580 gubar of cereal, perhaps 159,116 quintals; c) 118,715 sheep and 11,401 head of cattle; d) 1,500 minas of gold, that is 705 kgs, and 4,300 minas of silver: 2,021 kgs. But there is no mention either of the silver deposited in the treasury, é-siki ("house of the wool"), nor of the textile production, one of the most important economic activities of Ebla.

Obviously, this document is an important summary, but partial in any case, of the goods belonging to the Palace, recorded according to criteria that totally escape us.

Fields: The 422,000 measures GÁNA-ki of Idanekimu's fields (section [1]), constitute perhaps the largest area recorded in the tablets from Ebla. That prince, probably the son of Irkab-Damu, the penultimate king of Ebla, therefore had important organizational responsibilities. A lengthy summary of agricultural areas destined for the maintenance of some categories of Palace dependents, partly of low rank but certainly numerous, gives a total of 229,640 units, slightly more than half of all the fields controlled by Idanekimu. Some detailed data of this text, TM.75.G.10039, are (obv. I 1-IV 3): "157,500 measures for nourishing (kú) the workers (guruš); 11,860 measures for nourishing the officials ur$_4$; 21,230 measures for nourishing the carpenters (nagar) of the Palace; 10,920 measures for nourishing the Elders."

Quantifying these areas means formulating hypotheses, since the size of the unit of measure, GÁNA-ki, is not known. It has been suggested that it represents 1/10 of the

[19] See *ARES* I, p. 244.

[20] See *ARES* I, p. 223.

[21] See *ARES* I, p. 234.

Mesopotamian iku, that is 0.3528 hectares.[22] The allotments of individual low-ranking dependents are frequently of 200, and sometimes of 500 GÁNA-ki; and a field of 200 GÁNA-ki also generally entails the allotment of a pair of draught animals. If 1 GÁNA-ki corresponds to 352.8 m^2, we arrive at fields of 7 and 17.64 hectares, respectively, dimensions that are quite probable for a region in which dry agriculture was practiced.[23] TM.75.G.10217 records some areas near villages in the region of *Du-ne-íb*^{ki} (Tunip) for a total of 151,020 GÁNA-ki, that is 5,328 hectares, accepting the value of 352.8 m^2 per unit. The 422,000 GÁNA-ki under the control of Idanekimu would correspond, then, to 14,888 hectares, that is 15 km^2.

Barley: The quantities of barley are: 464,000 measures *gubar* of Idanekimu, in addition to 10,060 *gubar* of sig$_{15}$ cereal, in section (3); 100,000 of the king, in (7); 221,520 of the three overseers of Sisi, in (8); for a total of 795,580 units of measure. Only in TM.75.G.1700 (and in its duplicate 10228+10262) is a higher sum reached, which seems to be the total quantity of barley the Palace had at its disposal annually: 1,561,796 *gubar*, comprised of 501,866 *gubar* of the "hill," du$_6$-ki, 855,530 of the "surrounding centers," uru-bar, and 204,400 of the "overseers of the farmers of the king," ugula engar en.[24] Our document therefore seems to record approximately half of the total production or annual supply, even if we must consider the fluctuations to which the harvests were subject from year to year.

The *gubar* has a capacity of 20 nig-sagšu, and 1 nig-sagšu corresponds to 1 sìla, which is the measure for liquids. If the sìla of Ebla corresponds to the Mesopotamian one, which has a capacity of approximately 1 liter,[25] 1 *gubar* measures 20 liters. Idanekimu probably controlled 92,800 quintals of barley and 2,012 of sig$_{15}$ cereal. Calculating the production of barley per hectare at 10 quintals, which, however, could only be achieved in favorable years, these 94,812 quintals represent the production of 9,481 hectares, which is 63.7% of the 14,880 hectares calculated for Idanekimu (corresponding to 422,000 GÁNA-ki). Considering, instead, the production per hectare at 5.5 quintals of barley, which is more probable, the quantity of cereals represents the production of 17,238 hectares, that is, more than those calculated for Idanekimu.[26] The ratio between 98,812 quintals and 14,880 hectares is 6.64 quintals per hectare. In this case, fields in fallow cycle were not taken into account.

---

[22] F. Pomponio, *OLP* 14 (1983), pp. 5-12.

[23] Cfr. Archi, in *Mélanges P. Garelli*, Paris 1991, pp. 211-214, where surfaces planted with olive trees are detailed.

[24] TM.75.G.1700 is published by Archi in: *AfO* Beiheft 19 (1982), p. 182. The duplicate shows that in rev. I 1 (not very clear) one has to read 8 (and not 10, as it is given in the edition) *ma-i-at*.

[25] According to another less used system, the *gubar* was divided into 24 nig-sagšu, see L. Milano, *ARET* IX, pp. 349-350. Milano considers the an-zam (a submultiple of both the sìla and of the nig-sagšu in the ratio of 6:1), having the capacity of one liter. If that should hold true, that is 1 sìla = 6 liters, one obtains enormous amounts.

[26] T.J. Wilkinson, *Iraq* 51 (1989), p. 19, writes: "Modern Jazira systems...provide in most years only relatively modest yields of less than 1,000 kg per hectare and still represent a risky undertaking in dry years." However, today the fields are worked with tractors!

The 1,561,796 *gubar* in TM.75.G.1700 and 10228+10262 would correspond to 312,360 quintals, that is, the production of 31,236 or 56,793 hectares, at the ratio respectively of 10 and 5.5 quintals per hectare.

A standard typology of documents giving global data does not exist, and this makes it difficult to understand how the administration of this sector was organized. On the one hand, there are rather long lists of villages, with a quantity of barley for each village. TM.75.G.1621 lists only four villages, each to which are attributed 1,000 *gubar* of barley (which correspond to 200 quintals); evidently the amount of the production that was delivered to the Palace, perhaps as tribute of the community of villages. In any case, 1,000 *gubar* seems to be a minimum quantity. In TM.75.G.2036, the barley delivered by two villages in one year (1 mu) amounts to 7,510 *gubar* (375.5 quintals). On the other hand, some tablets give the quantities of barley "withdrawn," e_{11}, by some officials, without naming from where they come, so it is not possible to correlate these documents with the lists of villages. In general, it is a matter of some tens of thousands of *gubar*, TM.75.G.1883 obv. I 1-3: 60,140 *gú-bar* še e_{11} lú 2 šu *Šu-a-ḫu-lu*; 1972 obv. I 1-III 3: 34,760 *gú-bar* še e_{11} 47,515 *gú-bar* še nu-e_{11}...*áš-da Šu-ma*-NI. In TM.75.G.2677 one IrNE receives from another 13 or 14 lower officials 242,080 *gubar* (48,416 quintals);[27] similar is TM.75.G.10068, where each of 18 officials delivers from 1,000 to 11,000 *gubar*.

Sheep and cattle: The number of animals attributed to the king in section (5) is: 64,515 sheep, 9,941 heads of cattle besides 760 young cows. The 54,200 sheep in section (10) which "the king has taken into possession," en šu-du_8, must be other animals to be added to those in (5). In this way a total of 118,715 head is reached. In the previous text, the number of the sheep at the disposition of the king and the vizier does not turn out to be much smaller, 92,700, whereas the head of adult cattle number only 1,410, and the calves 1,000. The difference in the number of sheep could be explained as due to yearly variations, which are inevitable. It is more difficult to justify such a large difference for the cattle.

A larger number of sheep is found only in TM.75.G.1700 (10228+10262 is a duplicate of it), which seems to give a global summary of the Palace's movable property: 138,620 heads, whereas those of the cattle amount to 8,770 head.[28] In general, however, the numbers are lower. The texts recording the sheep qualified as "tribute for the king," igi-du_8, en, give the following totals:[29]

> TM.75.G.1574: 84,250 sheep; TM.75.G.1582: 72,710 [+10,000(?)] sheep;
> TM.75.G.2112: 72,240 sheep.

But already within the last of these texts a distinction is made between animals received as "tribute for the king," igi-du_8 en, and animals "taken in possession," šu-du_8. The

[27] Text published by Archi, in: *AfO* Beiheft 19 (1982), pp. 182-184.

[28] See note 24.

[29] The texts are all published, except TM.75.G.2554, by Archi, *SEb* 7 (1984) in the following pages: TM.75.G.1574, no. 17, pp. 68-69; 1582, no. 18, p. 69; 1845, no. 21, pp. 71-72; 2112, no. 20, pp. 70-71; 2222, no. 19, pp. 69-70; 1558, no. 10, pp. 63-64; TM.76.G.712, no. 16, pp. 67-68.

subsequent documents attribute the qualification of "tribute," igi-du$_8$, only to a portion of the animals:

TM.75.G.1845: 79,300 sheep, of which 51,810(?) as igi-du$_8$ en;
TM.75.G.2222: 67,060 sheep, of which 53,700 as igi-du$_8$ en;
TM.75.G.2554: 56,140, of which 37,100 as igi-du$_8$ en.

The sheep in section (5) seem to correspond to those that are classified as "tribute for the king" in these documents.[30]

The data regarding the cattle, section (5), are drawn from a detailed document concerning the "overseers of the cattle," TM.75.G.10213, which was preserved in the central archive L.2769. In it, a count is made of the cattle belonging to the king, estimating them according to the standard value of silver. This is a custom well known to the Eblaite administration, whose accounting implications are yet to be studied in detail.[31] The final value reached in the count, together with the total number of animals, is that included in section (5). The scribe of our text number 2, however, made an error: instead of 9,941 head of cattle, he wrote 9,741 (7 *mi-at* instead of 9 *mi-at*), later correcting himself sloppily by adding, when the tablet was already dry, two additional units that are scarcely visible. The two units can be identified only from the duplicate.

TM.75.G.10213: (obv. I 1) [x *mi-a*]*t* [x +] 3 ma-na bar$_6$:kù / lú gu$_4$-gu$_4$ ugula-ugula / ⌜ká-ká⌝ / [...] (II 1) [x +] 40 ma-na bar$_6$:kù / lú tu-da-*sù* / al$_6$-gál / é-siki / *ap* / 96 ma-na bar$_6$:kù / GIŠ-íb bar$_6$:kù / (III 1) ⌜gu$_4$-gu$_4$⌝ / *al*$_6^?$ / ugula-ugula / ká-ká / *wa* / *al*$_6$ / ugula gu$_4$-gu$_4$ / nu-ì-na-sum / é en / AN.ŠÈ.GÚ 3 *mi-at* 90 lá-1 ma-na (IV 1) [b]ar$_6$:[kù] / níg-s[a$_{10}$] 9 *l*[*i-im*] 9 *mi-at* 41 gu$_4$ / *ap* / 76 ma-na bar$_6$:kù / šu-bal-ak / (rev. I 1) 25 ma-na šú-ša kù-gi níg-[sa$_{10}$] 6 [+1 *mi-at*] 60 á[b-peš] / *in*[(-x)] / *si*-⌜x⌝ / ⌜*sù*⌝-*m*[*a*(x)] / (II 1) ugula gu$_4$-gu$_4$

"(obv. I 1-II 4) [x +] 103 minas of silver (value) of the cattle, the overseers of the administrative sectors [... ; x +] 40 minas of silver (value) of the (new) births are deposited in the 'house of wool' (i.e., the treasury).

(II 5-III 9) Further, 96 minas of silver, balance[32] of the silver of the cattle, (are) in the account of the overseers of the administrative sectors and in the

---

[30] Some texts record flocks entrusted to "head shepherds" ugula-mùnsub: 67,200 head in TM.75.G.1558, divided into 22 flocks in an equal number of villages. And again, 67,050 sheep in TM.76.G.712, "entrusted to EnnaNI and the head shepherds." The number of sheep is analogous to that of the "tributes to the king," but it is uncertain whether they were the same animals.

[31] The value of the "young cows" is given in gold. For the value of the wine stocked in the cellar, see below, 5.4.

[32] GIŠ-íb has the equivalence ᵓ*a*$_x$(NI)-*ḫir-tum* in the lexical lists, whose meaning as "remainder, balance" (cfr. Akk. *rēḫtum*) has been explained by Fronzaroli, *QdS* 13, pp. 121-122, and 134.

account of the overseer of the cattle (and) have not been given to the king's house.

(IV 1-rev. II 1) Total: 389 minas of silver, value of 9,941 heads of cattle; further 76 minas of silver to be changed in 25.20 minas of gold, value of 760 young cows...the overseer of the cattle."

The total estimate of 389 minas (182.83 kgs) of silver for 9,941 head of cattle, that is 2.34 shekels per animal (1 mina = 60 shekels; 1 shekel = 7.83 grs), is a low amount that can be explained if calves were also included among those animals. The value of a bovine could vary from 1 mina to 3 shekels.[33]

The colophon also documents the custom, rather frequent at Ebla, of evaluating the degree of purity of gold in comparison to silver.[34] The most refined gold had a ratio of 1:5 to silver, which is very low if compared to those documented in Mesopotamia during all its periods. Here it is a question of low-grade gold, which has a ratio of 1 : 3 to silver (1.520 shekels of gold : 4.560 shekels of silver). A "young cow," áb-peš, was therefore worth six shekels of silver, a price lower than that of 8.75 shekels given in *ARET* VII 74 (6). This calculation between gold and silver makes it probable that on occasion gold, instead of goods in kind, was paid to the administration.

Gold and silver: Section (11) gives one of the largest quantities of gold recorded in the archives of Ebla: 1,500 minas, equal to 705 kgs[35] "value," níg-sa_{10}, referring to *ba-rúm*, which is a difficult term to explain.[36]

Še-SAG×ḪA-mul, in sections (13) and (14) is "debt with interest." The lexical lists A, B, and D have: še-šu-ḫa-mul = *ḫu-bù-lu-um* (A), *ḫu-bù-lum*, *ḫu-*bu_x(NI)*-lum*, followed by: še-SAG×ḪA-mul, another spelling of the same word,[37] without equivalence. In the

[33] See Archi, *SEb* 7 (1984), p. 56.

[34] See H. Waetzoldt, *LdE*, p. 368; F. Pomponio, *AfO* 29-30 (1983/84), p. 62; *ARET* VII, pp. 224-225.

[35] Very high amounts of gold are registered, e.g., in TM.75.G.1908 rev. III, see Archi in *AfO* Beiheft 19 (1982), pp. 173 and 179.

[36] As it is said above, the Eblaite administration used to evaluate goods according to a silver standard; however, sometimes the value is given in gold, as here in section (5) for the "young cows."

It seems difficult to identify *ba-rúm* with baḫār-um/ "to choose," see igi-zàg = *ba-ʾà-lu-um, ba-ʾà-lum* in the lexical lists; *ba-i-la/ra-tum* is derived from this verb (see Fronzaroli, *QdS* 13, p. 137. One does not expect a personal name after níg-sa_{10}, and people having a name similar to *ba-rúm*, as Ba_4-LUM, *ARET* II 24 I 4; *Ba-lu*, *ARET* IV 23 rev. IV 6; *Ba-li*, *ARET* III 186 III, do not seem to have been responsible for acquiring goods for such a high value.

[37] On še-SAG×ḪA-mul see M. Civil, *BiOr* 40 (1983) p. 564.

administrative documents še-SAG×ḪA-mul refers to silver, barley and textiles.[38] Here no further element is given on the use of this silver.

Wood: To Ibbi-Zikir, the vizier, are ascribed important amounts of boxwood, GIŠ-taškarin, and scented wood of *cedar*, GIŠ-ir:nun, valued at 799 kgs of silver. The lexical lists have: ir-nun = *ar-gú-um* "scented resin," to be compared with Akkadian *argānu*, a conifer and its resin, whose Sumerian equivalence is giš-šim-ár-gan-nu,[39] while ir corresponds to Akkadian *armannu* and *erē/tšu*.[40] ir-nun is attested also in an inscription of UruKAgina,[41] in *IAS* 328 V 12' and 375 2'.[42] ì-ir-nun "oil perfumed with scented resin" is found in the hymn *ARET* V 6 iv 2 (ì-ir-nun giš:ì làl; dpl. *IAS* 326 III 1 is not clear) and in Statues C III 9, E III 14, F III 4 of Gudea.[43] Perfumed oil, ì-giš-ir, is mentioned also in the economic texts from Ebla.[44] Here, in section (15), GIŠ-ir-nun is understood as wood of the conifer from which the resin is derived, because it follows GIŠ-taškarin.

GIŠ-taškarin is associated with cedar both in Statue B of Gudea (III 28-35: GIŠ-erin, from the Amanus mountains) and in the building-inscription of Jaḫdun-Lim of Mari (II 14-18: "Il pénétra dans les Montagnes des Cèdres (GIŠ-erin) et de Buis (GIŠ-taškarin), montagnes élevées; du buis, du cèdre, du cyprés (GIŠ-šu-úr-man), et du bois de *l'élammakkum*, ces arbres il coupa)."[45]

The Eblaite lexical lists have GIŠ-nun-sal = *ar-za-tum*,[46] and GIŠ-nun-ir = *ar-gúm*, *i-tum*. A scented oil is obtained from its essence, which is quoted in the ritual for the enthronement of king and queen, TM.75.G.1823 + : ì-giš GIŠ-*i-du-um*, parallel text 1939+: ì-gis GIŠ-*ir-dè*, that is /HirD-um/, with omission of /r/ both in the first text as well as in the gloss.[47] Because *arzatum* seems to be the word for "fir,"[48] GIŠ-nun-ir could mean "cedar."

---

[38] See *ARET* VII, p. 233, and add TM.75.G.1475, which has four entries built according to the following scheme: "x barley present, x barley given as loan at interest: PN" x *gú-bar* še al$_6$-gál x *gú-bar* še ì-na-sum še-SAG×ḪA-mul PN. The amounts are:

	gú-bar še al$_6$-gál	*gú-bar* še ì-na-sum še-SAG×ḪA-mul
1)	4,150	4,300
2)	5,270	2,500
3)	600	350
4)	1,200	800

[39] Fronzaroli, *SEb* 7 (1984), pp. 149-150. For *arganu* (already attested in Old Akkadian, see I.J. Gelb, *MAD* 3, p. 63), see *AHw*, p. 67a; *CAD* A, II, pp. 253-254.

[40] See *AHw*, p. 242; *CAD* E, p. 280.

[41] Cfr. H. Behrens - H. Steible, *Glossar zu den altsumerischen Bau- und Weihinschriften*, (FAOS 6), Wiesbaden 1983, p. 177.

[42] See J. Bauer, *Altorientalischen Notizien* 9 (1980), p. 2.

[43] Deimel, ŠL II,2, p. 471. For ì-ir-a, see J. Bauer, *Altsumerische Wirtschaftstexte aus Lagasch*, Rom 1972, p. 334.

[44] 129 jars, la-ḫa, of ì-giš-ir are attested in TM.75.G.1536 rev. II 4, see Archi, *AoF* 13 (1986) p. 197.

[45] G. Dossin, *Syria* 32 (1955), pp. 13-14.

[46] See Fronzaroli, *SEb* 1 (1979), p. 67; Id., *QdS* 13, p. 136; M. Krebernik, *ZA* 73 (1983), p. 17.

[47] See Fronzaroli, *NABU* 1989/2.

[48] See *HAL*, p. 83b.

In order to appreciate what the value of this boxwood and cedarwood as 799 kgs (1,700 minas) of silver meant for the Eblaite economy, one has to keep in mind that according to this document 183 kgs (389 minas) was the value of 9,941 old and young head of cattle, and 35.7 kgs of silver that of 760 young cows (section [5]). The 1,500 minas of gold in section (11), at a ratio of 1:3 with silver, mean 2,115 kgs of silver—that is the value of 114,891 head of cattle!

3. Wine Deliveries

The tablets numbered 3 and 4 record lists of deliveries of wine in jars, for a general total of more than 200 units. Documents of this kind were not kept in the central archive, L.2769. Instead there are registrations of incoming jars of wine (a few units each time), in general sent as gifts to the king himself. In exchange for these deliveries clothing is given, as in *ARET* III 90 II: "[x garments to PN for the delivery] of two jars of wine for the king and his mother"] 2 dug geštin en *wa* ama-gal-*sù*.[49]

In the documents of archive L.2712 (*ARET* IX and X), concerning the distribution of food products, deliveries of wine are very few, and only as an addition to cereal products, as well as to the "regular offerings," sá-du$_{11}$-ga, for the god Enki in *ARET* IX 107: "5 jars of wine, 14 sìla measures of wine...." 5 dug geštin 14 sìla geštin LAK-92 a (obv. IV 1-2), 8 sìla geštin LAK-92 a (obv. V 6-rev. I 2); or to the "regular offerings" for the goddess Išḫara, *ARET* X 90 rev. II 4-6: 4$^{?}$ dug LAK-92 a 2 dug geštin.

Perhaps the office where the bookkeeping pertaining to the wine collected in the Palace's storerooms was located in the vicinity of room L.3143.

Text no. 3: TM.82.G.265[50]
(Copy on Plates IV-V and photographs on Plates XII-XIII)

Obv.	I	1	6 dug geštin
			I-da-ne-ki-mu
		3	11 dug geštin
			A-ḪAR-*ar-mu*
		5	3 ⌈dug⌉ [gešt]in
			ʾÀ-da-ša
		7	*Ù-kul*^{ki}
			4[a)] dug geštin
		9	*Gi*$^{!}$*-rí*

---

[49] See below 5. However, a delivery of wine for the town of Nagar occurs in *ARET* VIII 542 (22): 2+2 garments *Bù-wa-mu A-bù*-NI maškim *Íl-zi* BE-é geštin wa ì-giš *si-in Na-gàr*^{ki}.

[50] The tablet was found on the floor of L.3143. It measures 120 × 150 mm.

		⌈2⌉ [dug geštin]
II	1	*Bar-za-ma-ù*
		2 dug geštin
	3	*I-t*[*i*]-NI
		3 dug geštin
	5	*A-bu*
		1 dug geštin
	7	en
		Ì-mar^{ki}
	9	1 dug geštin
		Šu-NI-LUM
	11	1 dug geštin
		Du-na-ù
	13	[x du]g geštin
		[x-N]I$^{?}$-LUM
	15	3 dug geštin
III	1	[x-*d*]*a*-[N]I
		lú *A*-NE-⌈u_9⌉
	3	⌈2⌉ dug geštin
		Ar-šè-a-ḫu
	5	lú *A*-NE-ʾ*à*
		2 dug geštin
	7	*Bù-da*-NI
		lú *A*-NE-ʾ*à*
	9	2 dug geštin
		Puzur$_4$*-ra-ma-lik*
	11	10 dug geštin
		3 *Sá*-⌈*mu*⌉
	13	(uninscribed) MU
IV	1	[x du]g geštin
		Puzur$_4$*-ra*-BE
	3	nag
		in lú
	5	*I-da-ne-ki-*[*m*]*u*
		1 dug geštin
	7	*B*[*ù-*]*la*
		si-in
	9	*Ši-sal*^{ki}
		in
	11	lú *I-da-ne-ki-mu*
		2 dug geštin
	13	*in*
		lú *I-da-ne-ki-mu*
	15	2 dug geštin

		in
V	1	*A*-ḪAR-*ar-mu*
		ᵓ*À-da-ša*
	3	lú *Na-mi*
		si-in
	5	*Ši-sal*^{ki}
		1 dug geštin
	7	*ma-lik-tum*
		in
	9	lú ⌈*I*⌉-[*d*]*a-ne-ki-mu*
		1 dug geštin
	11	é en
		Du-NE-*a*-NE
	13	šu-ba$_4$-ti
		in
	15	lú *I-da-ne-ki-mu*
		1 dug
	17	*Bù-la*
VI	1	*si-in*
		Ši-sal^{ki}
	3	1 dug geštin
		Du-NE-*a*-NE
	5	nag
		in
	7	⌈lú⌉ *I*-⌈*da*⌉-*ne-ki-mu*
		1 dug
	9	*Du*-NE-*a*-NE
		in
	11	lú
		Gi-rí
	13	é en
		áš-da
	15	kú
		mu-DU
VII	1	1 [dug] ge[štin]
		i[*n*]
	3	l[ú] *Gi*-[*rí*]
		D[*u-bí*]-*z*[*i-kir*](?)
	5	⌈x⌉[-
		U[R-
	7$^?$	NI[-
		1[+2$^?$ dug]
	9	*T*[*i*-(x-)]*m*[*a*(-x)]
		Bù[-

PLATES

Tablet 1

I III

Obv.

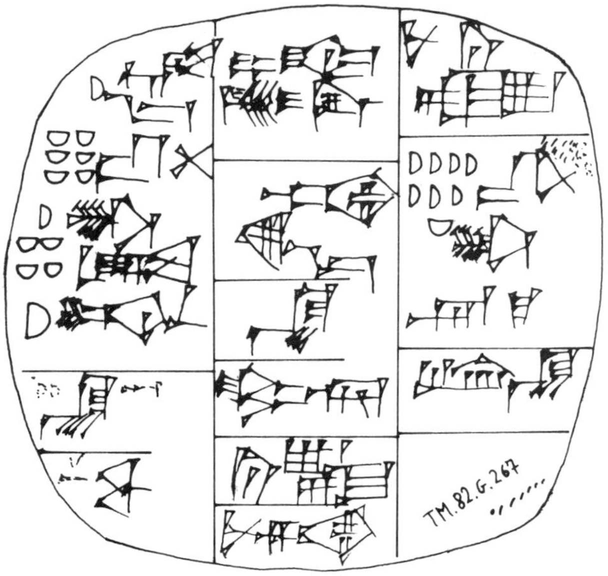

III I

Rev.

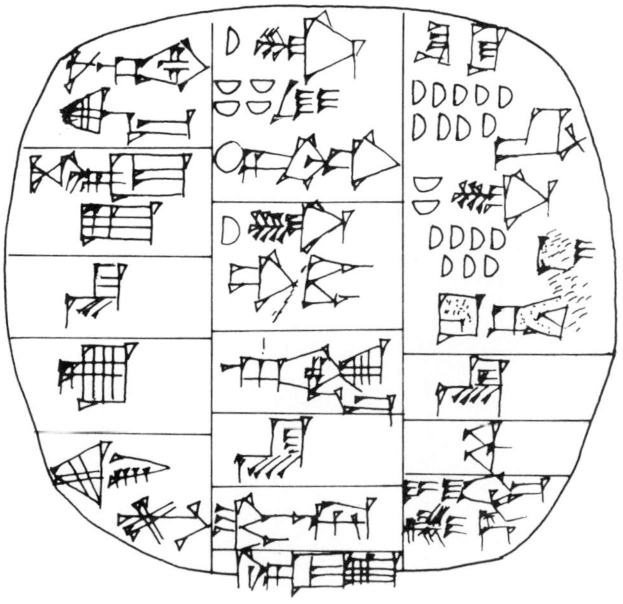

Tablet 2

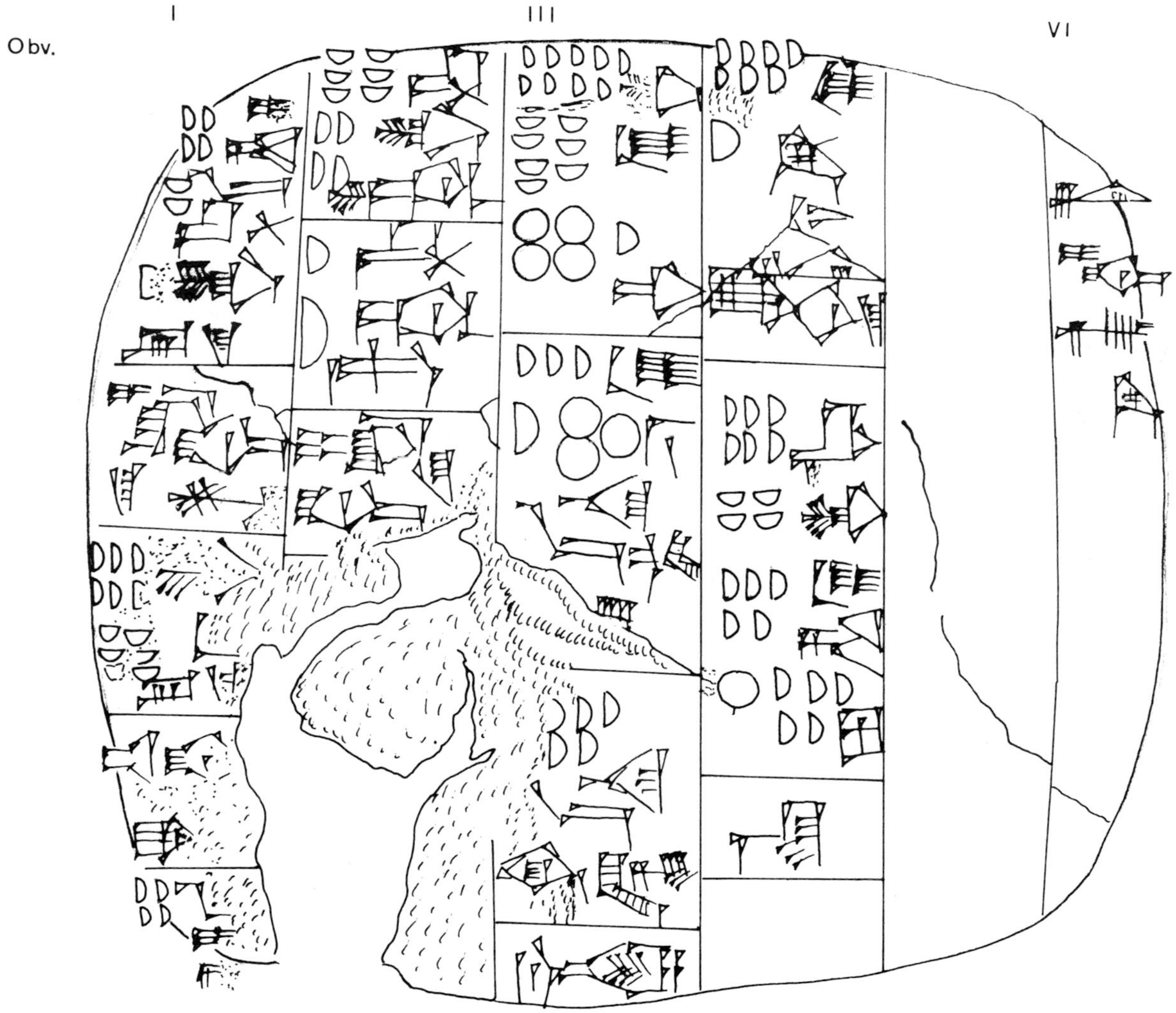

Tablet 2

Rev.

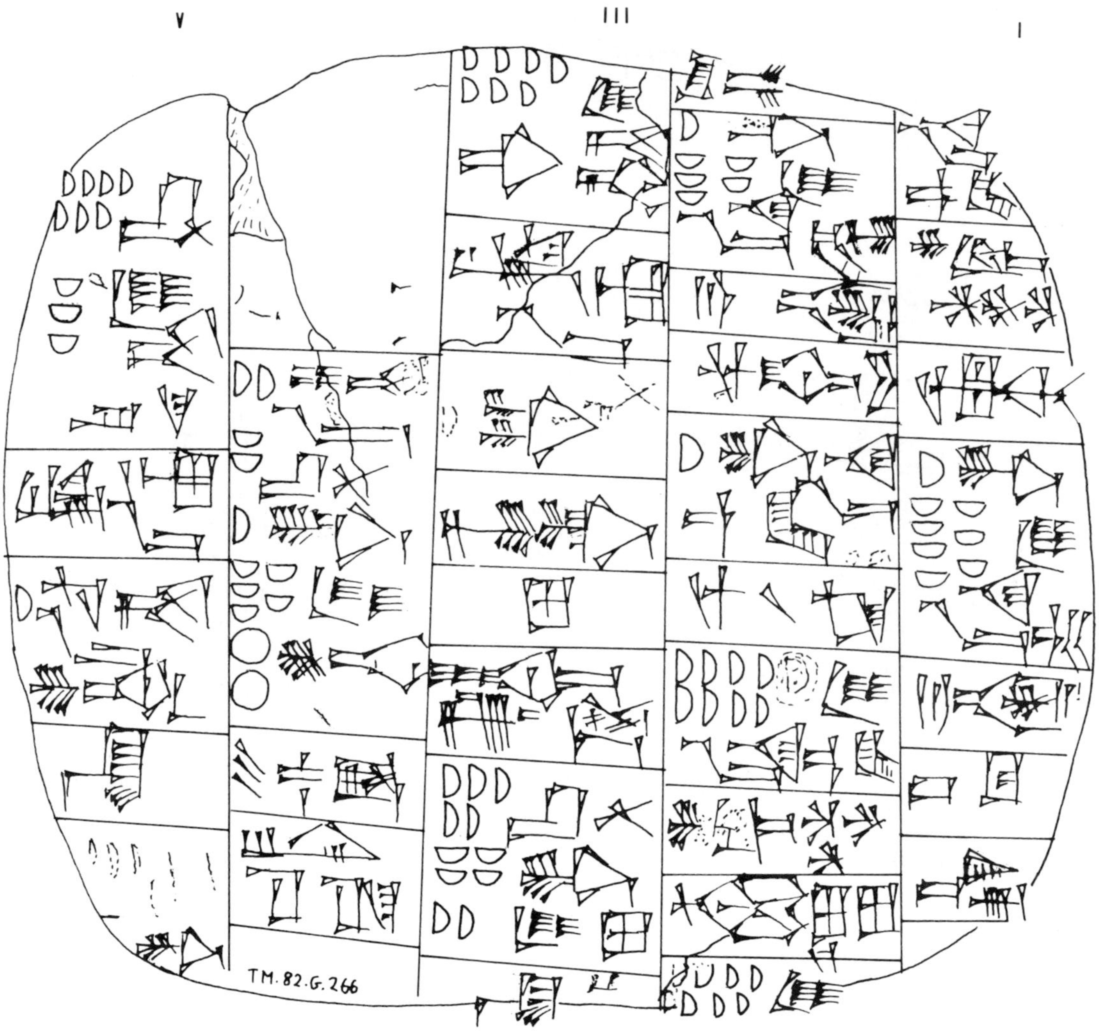

Tablet 3

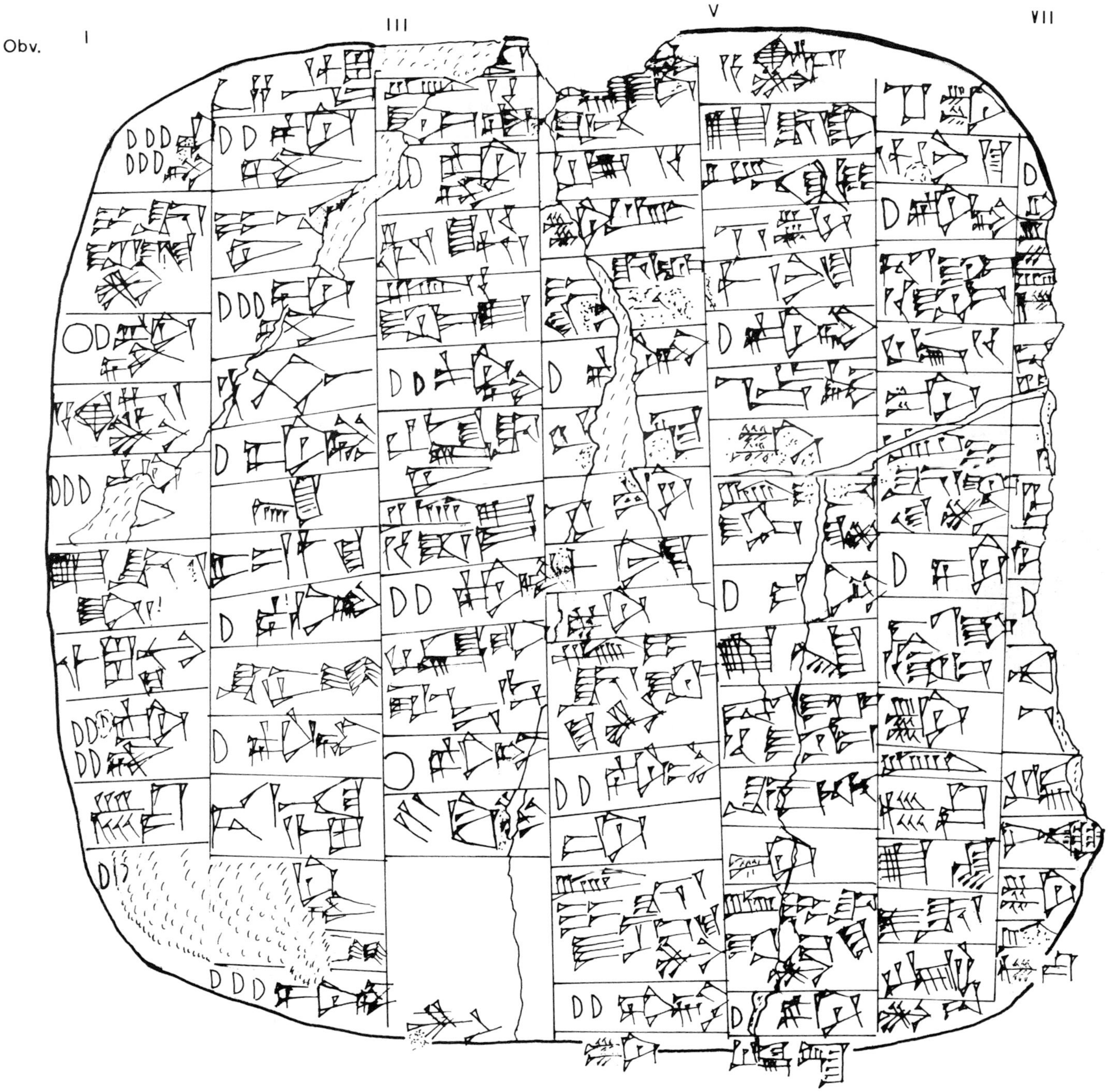

Tablet 3

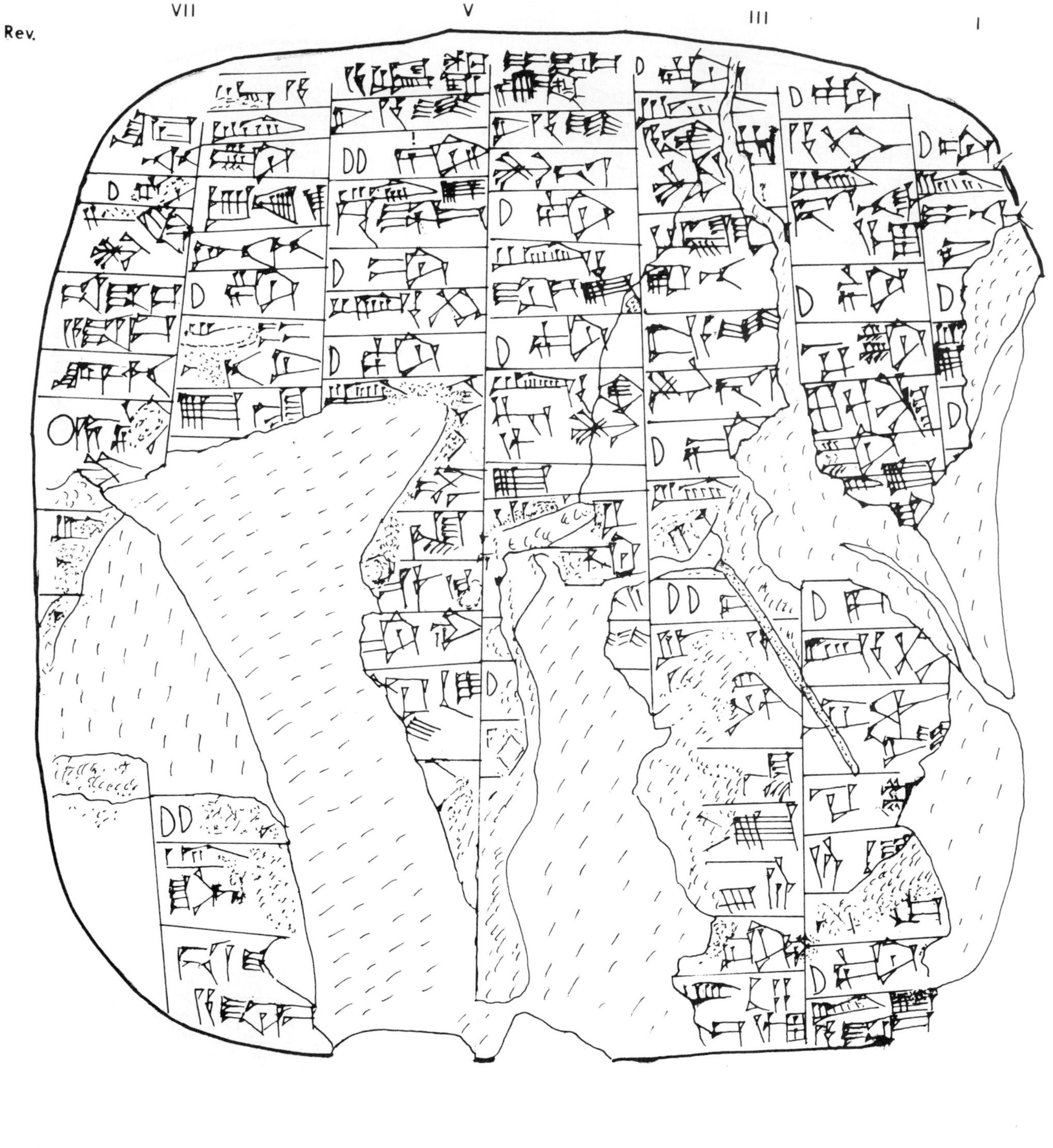

Tablet 4

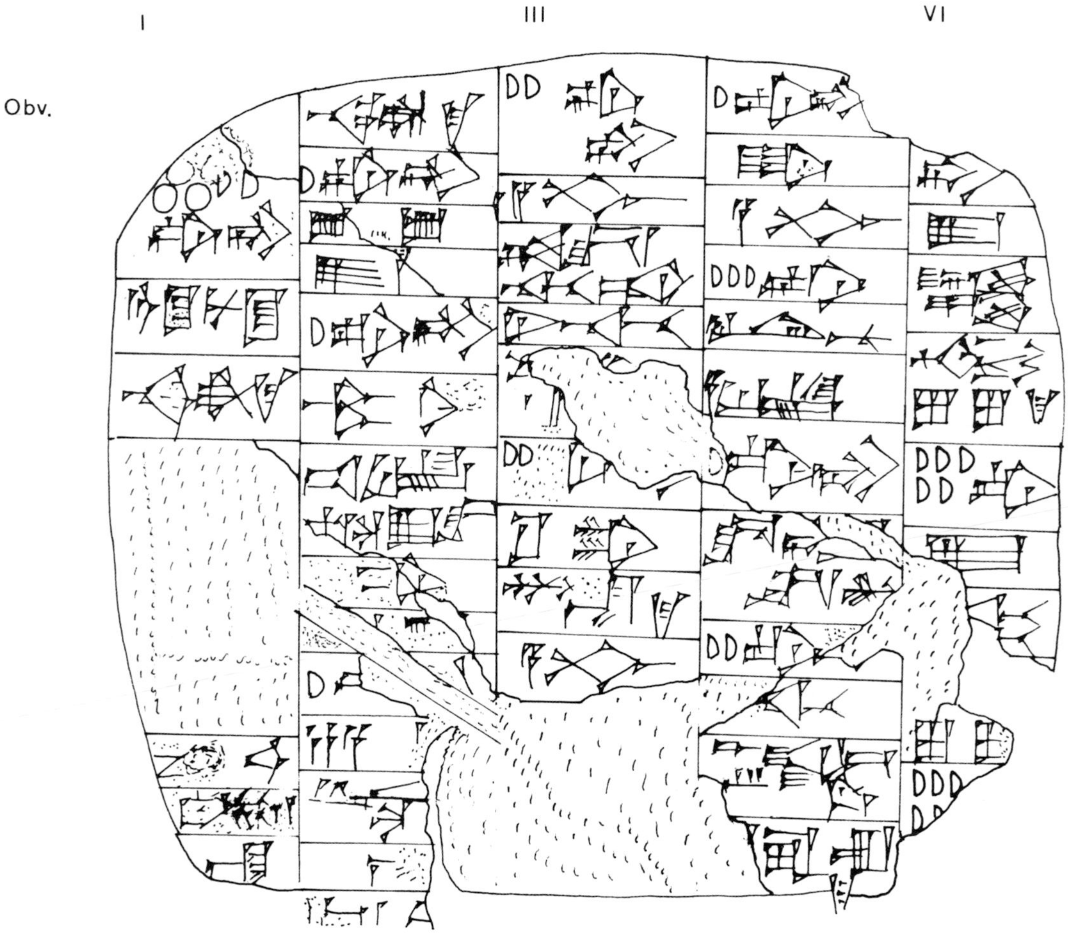

Tablet 4

Rev.

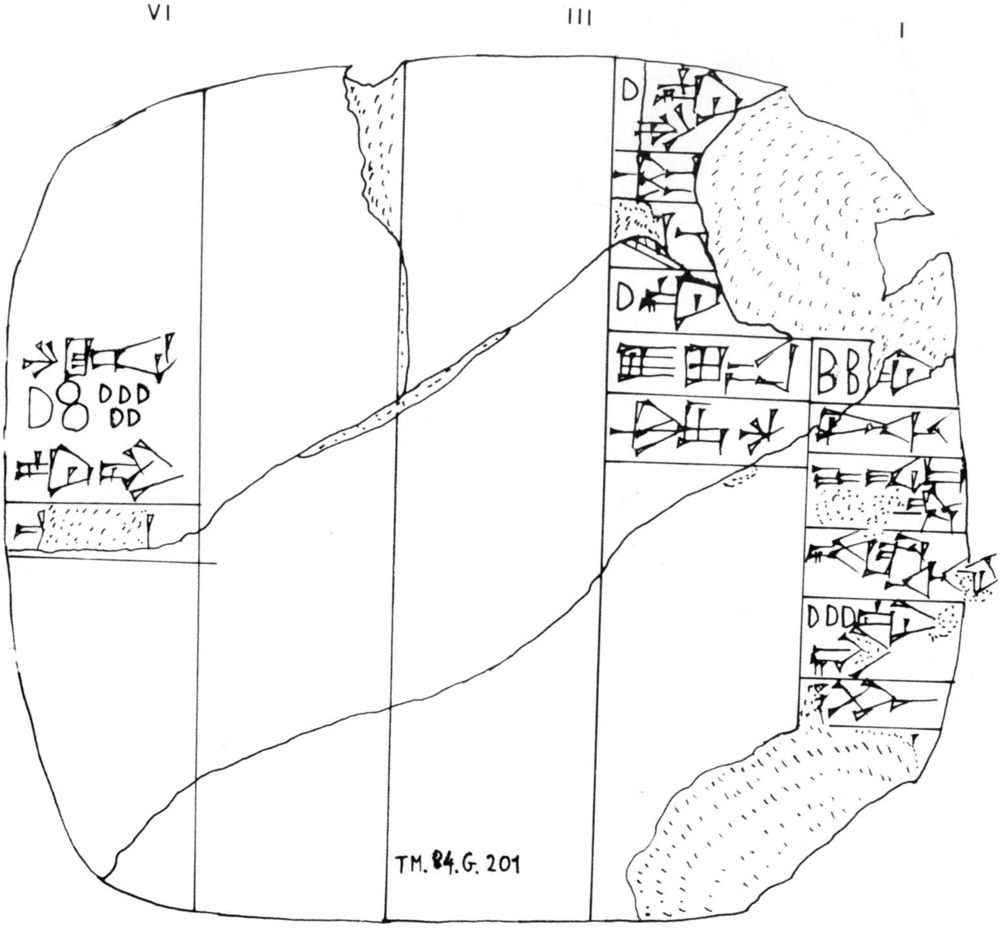

Tablet 5

Obv.

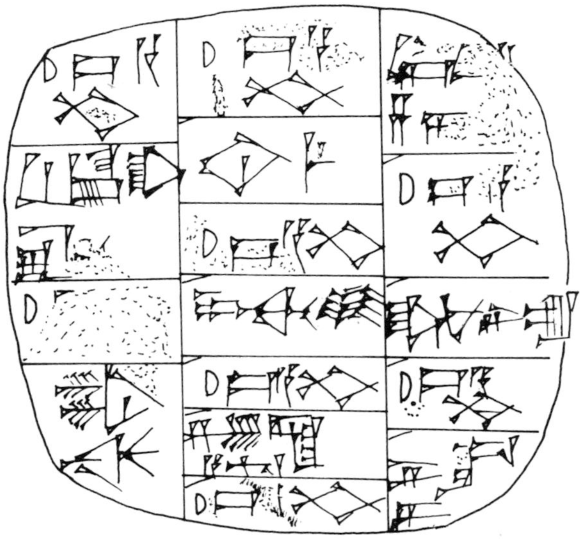

Rev

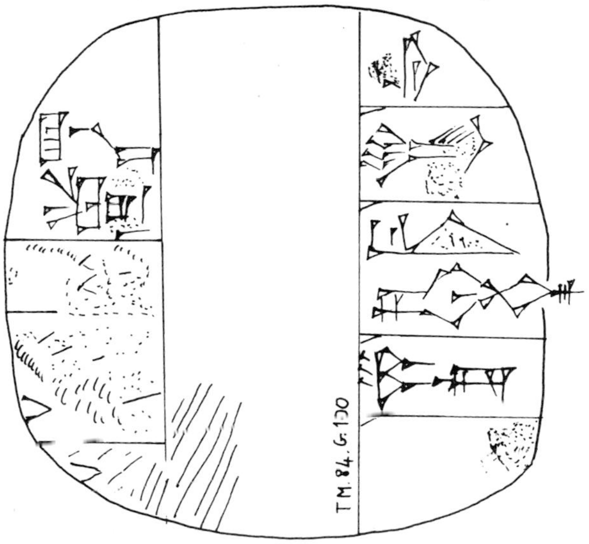

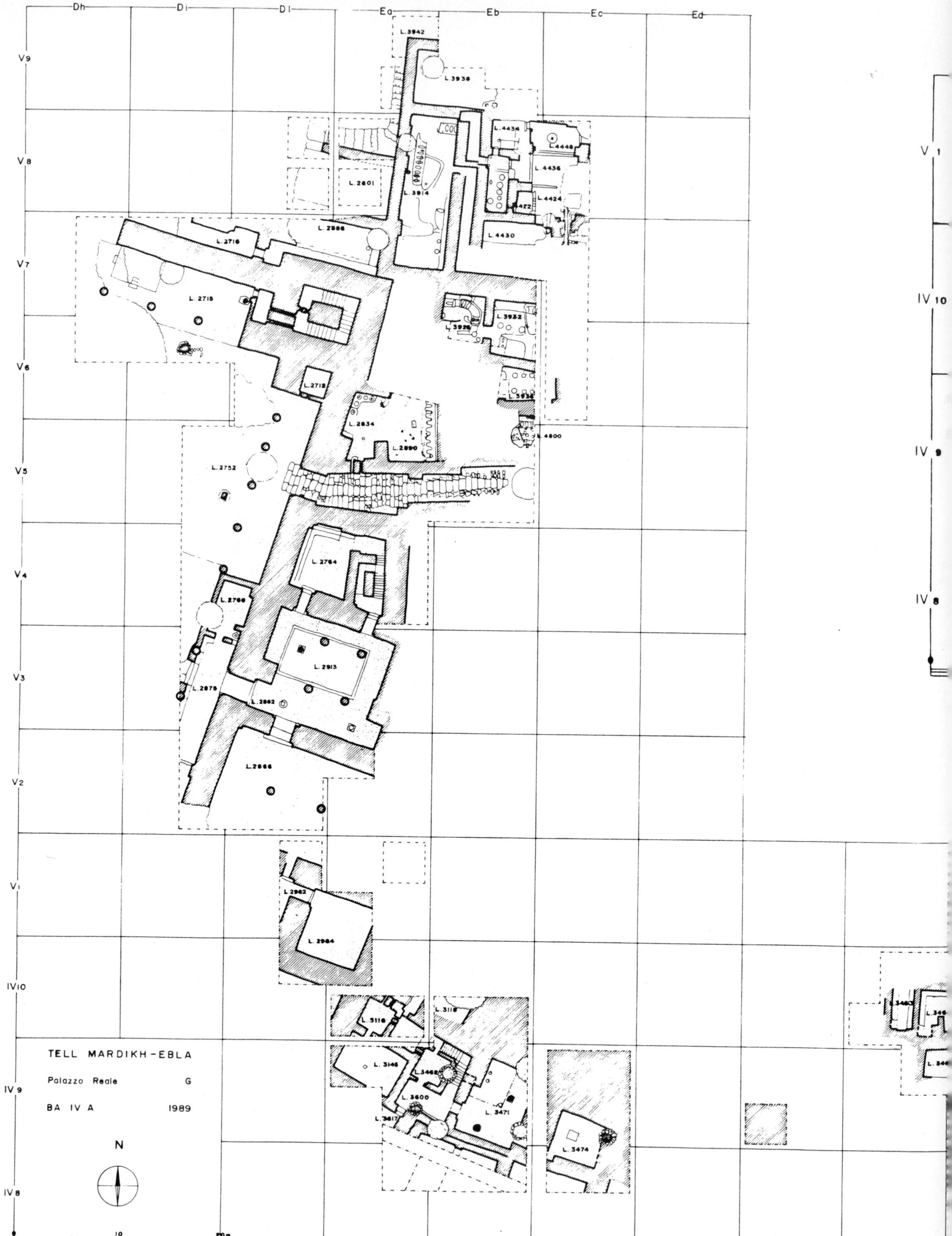

TELL MARDIKH-EBLA
Palazzo Reale G
BA IV A 1989
N
10
20m
L. 3942
L. 3938
L. 4434
L. 4448
L. 4436
L. 4424
L. 4422
L. 4430
L. 2601
L. 3914
L. 2586
L. 2716
L. 2715
L. 3932
L. 3926
L. 2712
L. 3934
L. 2834
L. 2890
L. 4800
L. 2752
L. 2764
L. 2766
L. 2913
L. 2875
L. 2862
L. 2866
L. 2982
L. 2984
L. 3116
L. 3118
L. 3145
L. 3462
L. 3600
L. 3617
L. 3471
L. 3474
Dh
Di
Dl
Ea
Eb
Ec
Ed
Ee
Ef
V9
V8
V7
V6
V5
V4
V3
V2
V1
IV10
IV9
IV8

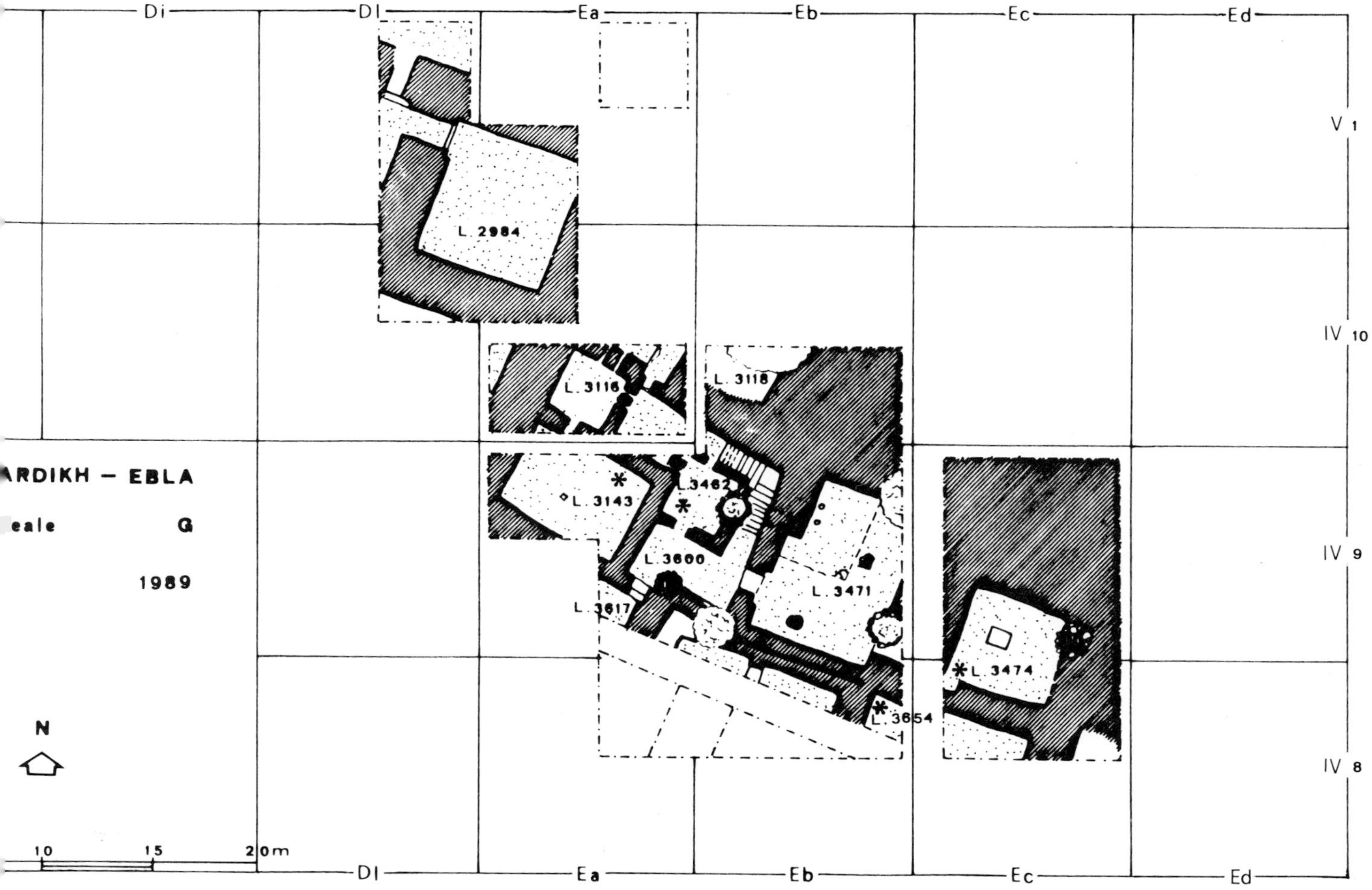

(figure 2)
Plan of the Southern Wing of Royal Palace G

(figure 1)
Plan of Royal Palace G

Tablet 1

obverse

obverse - upper edge

obverse - lower edge

reverse

reverse - upper edge

reverse - lower edge

Tablet 2

obverse

obverse - left edge

Tablet 2

reverse

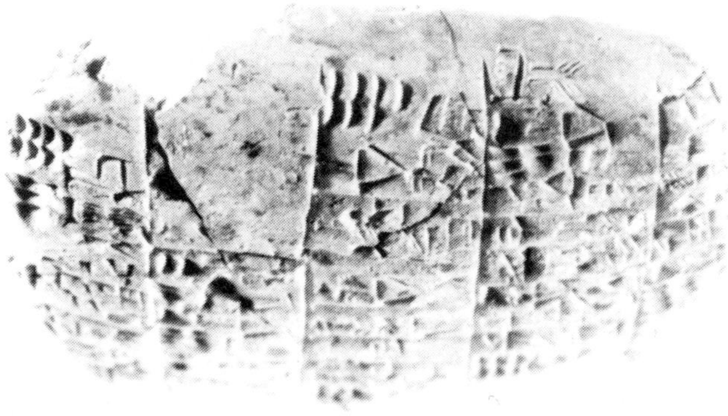

reverse-
upper edge

reverse-
right edge

reverse-
lower edge

Tablet 3

obverse -
upper edge

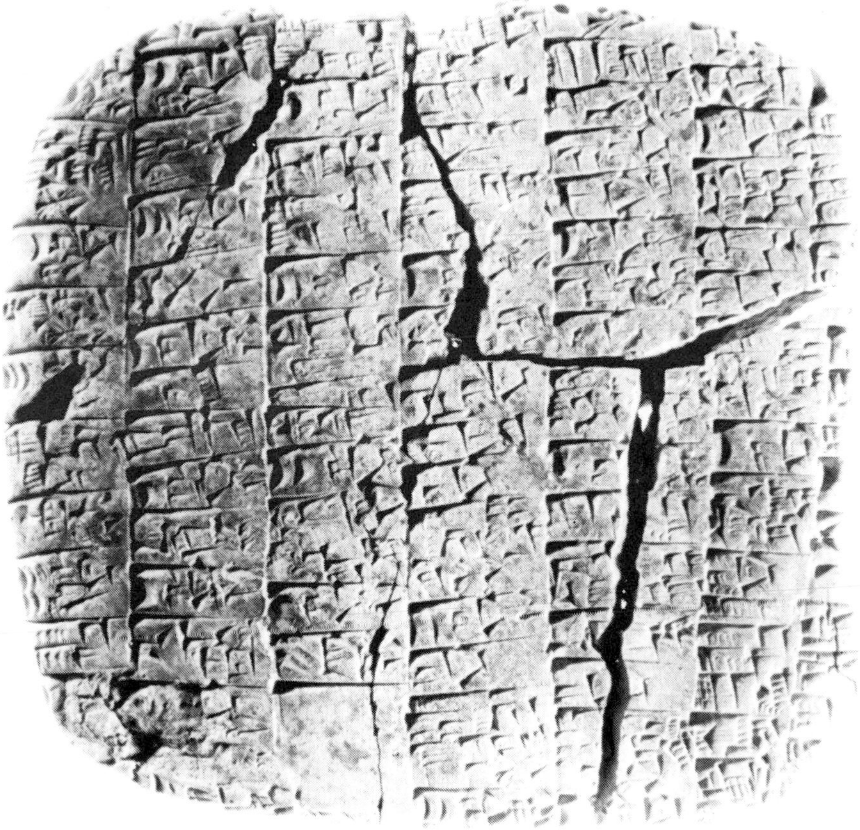

obverse

obverse-
lower edge

Tablet 3

reverse - left edge

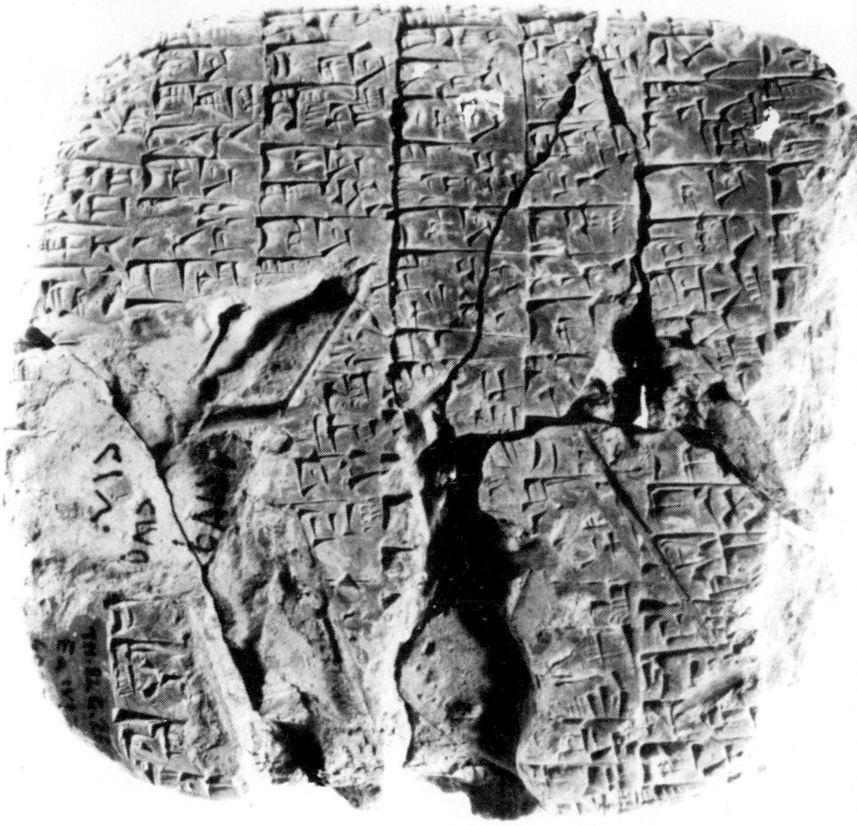

reverse

reverse - upper edge

reverse - lower edge

Tablet 4

obverse - upper edge

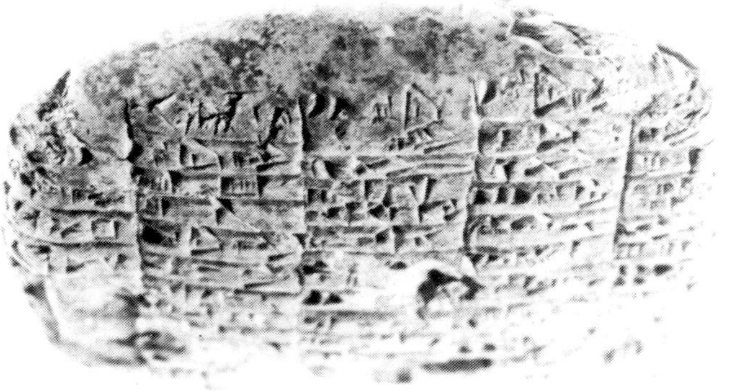

obverse

obverse - lower edge

Tablet 4

reverse

left edge

Tablet 5

obverse

reverse

		11	ì-na-sum
			in
		13	lú *Gi-rí*
Rev.	I	1	1 dug
			lú *I-ti*-NI
		3	1 d[ug]
			l[ú] ⸢*ʾÀ*⸣/*S*[*a*-
		5	1 [dug]
			[(about 10 cases)]
	II	1	1 dug
			A-bu
		3	lú *Du-na-ù*
			1 dug
		5	*si-in*
			Lu-ba-an^{ki}
		7	*in*
			[l]ú *ʾÀ*-[*d*]*a*-⸢*ša*⸣
		9	1 d[ug]
			lú$^{!}$ *A-bu*
		11	NI-PI-NI-L[UM]
			si-i[*n*]
		13	NÍG-M[I]$^{?}$ ⸢x⸣
			⸢x⸣-[N]E
		15	1 dug
			lú *A*-NE-*ʾà*
	III	1	1 dug
			lú *A*-ḪAR-*ar-mu*
		3	*Puzur*$_4$-*ra*-BE
			NI-*a*-LUM
		5	mu$^{!}$-DU
			1 dug
		7	lú ⸢x⸣[
			2 d[ug]
		9	⸢lú⸣ ⸢*A*⸣-⸢x⸣-⸢x⸣-⸢x⸣-⸢x⸣
			[x] en
		11	[*i*]*n* é
			⸢kú⸣
		13	[1] dug geštin
			[l]ú *Bar-za-ma-ù*
	IV	1	*I-bí-zi-kir*
			NI-*a*-LUM
		3	mu-DU
			1 dug
		5	lú *A*-NE-*ʾà*

		1 dug
	7	lú *A*-ḪAR-*ar-mu*
		é
	9	⌈x⌉-[*r*]*a*
		⌈kú⌉(?)
	11	[-L]UM
		1 [dug]
		[(about 5 cases)]
V	1	*A-bù-*^{d}*Ku-ra*
		NI-*a*-LUM
	3	2 dug
		lú *A*-NE-ʾ*à*
	5	1 dug
		lú *A-bu*
	7	1 dug
		lú [*A*-]⌈ḪAR⌉-[*ar-m*]*u*
	9	[1 dug] geštin
		en
	11	[*Ì*-]*mar*^{ki}
		[1] dug geštin
	13	[ ]*si*$^{?}$-*mi*[- -LU]M
		[ ]-⌈x⌉
	15	[(about 4 cases)]
VI	1	nag
		lú
	3	*in*
		Ib-su^{ki}
	5	ì-ti
		1 dug
	7	⌈lú⌉[b)] *I-ti*-NI
		é en
	9	[(about 6 cases)]
	15$^{?}$	2 [dug]
		lú [(x)] *Ša*-⌈x⌉[
	17	*Du*-N[E-]*a*-NE
VII	1	šu-ba$_4$-ti
		1 dug
	3	lú III *Sá-mu*
		Du-NE-*a*-NE
	5	šu-ba$_4$-ti
		10 lá-2 ⌈dug⌉ ⌈geštin⌉
	7	lú ⌈x⌉[
		⌈x⌉[
	9	[ ]

[ ]
(space uninscribed)

a) 1: erased, originally: 5.
b) Partly cancelled, probably wrongly.

This document registers deliveries of wine totaling more than 100 jars (to the 97 listed in the text one has to add about another dozen, taking into account the unpreserved cases). That corresponds to about 2,000 liters of wine if the dug had here the capacity of 20 sìla as in TM.75.G.1451 obv. VI 5-7.[51] Three jars are for the house of the king, é en, obv. V 11, VI 13, rev. VI 8, and the first two are entrusted to a certain DuNEaNE. Others are for the king of Emar (obv. II 7-8, rev. V 10-11). Among the numerous consignees there are Idanekimu, a "king's son" of the first generation (*ARES* I, 223), and Giri, perhaps a son of Ibrium (*ARES* I, 233). This does not necessitate a high date for the text. Ibbi-Zikir mentioned in rev. IV 1 has to be the last vizier, and Adaša from Ukul (obv. I 6-7) appears also in *ARET* I 5 obv. XV 9-10; VIII 521 IV 9-10; 534 XVII 7-8; 541 I 2-3, all tablets which belong to the lot found in the "Audience Hall" (L.2752), which are to be dated to the last period of Ebla.[52]

The notation: *in* lú PN "(to be charged) to what (is due) to PN" is frequent. It refers to Adaša, rev. II 7-8; Giri, obv. VI 10-12, VII 2-3, 12-13; Idanekimu, obv. IV 4-5: "[1] jar to PN for drinking (nag) (to be charged) to what (is due) to I," 10-11, 13-14, V 8-9, 14-15, VI 6-7.

Text no. 4: TM.84.G.201[53]
(Copy on Plates VI-VII and photographs on Plates XIV-XV)

Obv. I 1 ⌜42⌝ dug geštin
níg-šè-nu-šè
3 *Na-gàr*^{ki}
[ ]
5 [ ]
[ ]
7 *in* ud
⌜níg-mu-sá⌝ (?)
9 en

[51] See *SEb* 4 (1981), p. 7.

[52] When this text was published, it was thought that Ibrium was king of Ebla, and not a vizier. Therefore the dating proposed in *ARET* I, p. 58 is no longer valid. In this document, section (72), Irak-Damu is also mentioned, who plays the most important role (after the king and the queen) in the offering lists to the gods, all to be dated to the last period of Ebla. Four of these texts are published by G. Pettinato, *OA* 18 (1979), pp. 85-215. In *ARET* I 5 (61) and (58) Šura-Damu and Ze-Damu are mentioned, two "king's sons," respectively of the first and second generations.

[53] The tablet was found in room L.3474, 20 cm above the level of the floor. It measures 90 × 87 mm.

II	1	*Na-*⌈*gàr*⌉^{ki} .
		1 dug geštin
	3	ib-ib
		é
	5	1 dug geštin
		1 dumu-mí
	7	*Du-bù-ḫu-*$^{d>}$*À-da*
		⌈*in*⌉
	9	[x] ⌈x⌉ [(x)]
		1 d[ug gešt]in
	11	*Za-a-š*[*è*]
		l[ú] dingir[-dingir]
	13	e[n](?)
		⌈UR⌉? ⌈x⌉
III	1	2 dug geštin
		A-bu
	3	*Ad-da-ti-gú*$^{<ki>}$
		ì-ti
	5	⌈x⌉ ⌈x⌉ ⌈x⌉
		2 [d]ug [gešti]n
	7	*si-in*
		Mu-ru$_{12}^{ki}$
	9	*A-bu*
		[ ]
	11	[ ]
		[ ]
IV	1	1 dug gešt[in]
		ZA$_x$
	3	*A-bu*
		3 dug
	5	lú TIL
		A-bù
	7	⌈1⌉ dug geštin
		Da-kùn-Da-mu
	9	2 dug g[eštin]
		[ì-]ti
	11	*I-bí-zi-kir*
		[*D*]*a-ra-um*^{ki}
V	1	[1 dug] geštin
		é
	3	simug-simug
		Kam$_4$*-lu-lu*^{ki}
	5	5 dug
		é

		7	[nag]ar-[nag]ar
			[*Kam*$_4$*-*]*lu-l*[*u*^{ki}]
		9	5[+1 dug]
Rev.	I	1	[ ]
			[ ]
		3	[ ]
			4 ⌜dug⌝
		5	ì-ti
			I-bí-[*zi-*]*kir*
		7	*Ad-da-ti-*⌜*gú*⌝$^{!<ki>}$
			3 dug geštin
		9	⌜*A*⌝*-bu*
			[....]⌜x⌝[ ]
	II	1	1 dug geštin
			1 dumu-m[í]$^{?}$
		3	⌜*Iš*$_{11}$⌝*-m*[*a-ì/lik*]
			1 dug [geštin]
		5	*Sa-lu-du*
			1 dam dingir
		7	(uninscribed)
	III		(uninscribed)
	IV		(uninscribed)
	V	1	(space uninscribed) AN.ŠÈ.GÚ 85 dug geštin
			⌜è⌝
		3	(uninscribed)

Obv. I 1-II 1: 42 jars of wine packed for the town of Nagar [...] when the king of Nagar married(?).

II 2-4: 1 jar of wine for the ib-ib officials of the house.

II 5-9: 1 jar of wine for a daughter of Dubuḫu-Ada (son of vizier Ibbi-Zikir) for [...].

II 10-14: 1 jar of wine for Zaʾaše, (the devoted) to the god[s] of the king(?)[...].

III 1-5: 2 jars of wine when Abu was in the town of Addatigu.[54]

III 6-12: 2 jars of wine for the town of Muru, Abu [...].

IV 1-3: 1 jar of wine: property of Abu.

IV 4-6: 3 jars (*in restitution*) for what Abu had lost.

IV 7-8: 1 jar of wine for Dakun-Damu ("woman," dam, of Ibbi-Zikir).[55]

IV 9-12: 2 jars of wine (when) Ibbi-Zikir was in the town of Daraum.

V 1-4: [1 jar] of wine for the workshop of the carpenters of the town of Kamlulu.

V 5-8: 5 jars for the workshop of the carpenters of the town of Kamlulu.

V 9-Rev. I 3: 5 [+1 jars...]

---

[54] *Ad-da-ti-gú*$^{<ki>}$ is here understood as a variant writing of *A-da-ti-gú*^{ki}. Note in connection with the present passage *ARET* II 12 obv. V 3-8 wherein a certain *A-bu* receives garments in *A-da-ti-gú*^{ki}.

[55] See *ARES* I, p. 262.

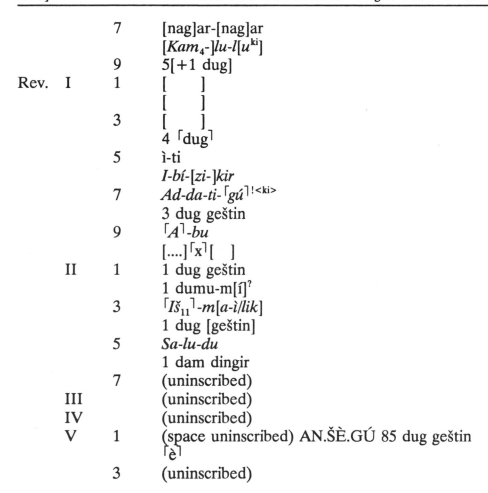

Rev. I 4-7: 4 jars when Ibbi-Zikir was in the town of Addatigu.
I 8-10: 3 jars of wine for Abu [...].
II 1-3: 1 jar for the daughter of Iš-Ma[i/lik].
II 4-5: 1 jar [of wine] for Saludu, the priestess.
V 1-2: Total: 85 jars of wine; disbursed.

4. Deliveries of wet malt

Text no. 5: TM.84.G.100[56]
(Copy on Plate VIII and photographs on Plate XVI)

Obv.	I	1	1 GIŠ-a-mùnu
			Puzur$_4$*-ra-*⌜BE⌝[a)]
		3	1 G[IŠ-a-mùnu]
			In-ti
	II	1	1 GIŠ-a-mùnu
			te:me
		3	1 GIŠ-a-mùnu
			I-ti-LUM
		5	1 GIŠ-a-mùnu
			Gi-la-a-ḫu
		7	1 GIŠ-a-mùnu
	III	1	*Ìr*[b)]*-za*-NI
			1 GIŠ-a-mùnu
		3	*Ša-nu*-NI-*um*
			1 GIŠ-a-mùnu
		5	NI-*da*-NI
Rev.	I	1	sur
			sa$_6$
		3	lú *al*$_6$*-sù*
			3[c)] dumu-nita
		5	(uninscribed)
	II		(uninscribed)
	III	1	*Šè-ma-*[d]*Ku-ra*
			(cancelled)
		3	(cancelled)
			(cancelled)

a) BE seems to have been unintentionally damaged, but the reading *Puzur*$_4$*-ra* is also possible.
b) *Ìr-* is written on an erased sign.
c) The three oblique signs are lightly engraved.

---

[56] The tablet was found beside the wall M.3652, in room L.3564. It measures 47 × 46 mm.

On the obverse, there were eight deliveries of GIŠ-a-mùnu to eight people. Šema-Kura, whose name occurs in rev. III 1, not followed by any administrative notation, seems to have supervised these deliveries. He has to be identified with the Šema-Kura "overseer of the property of (vizier) Ibbi-Zikir" (*Š.* ugula ZA_x *I.*, *ARET* VII 109). He is qualified as a maškim of Ibbi-Zikir [*ARET* IV 1 (4) and (78)]. TM.76.G.80 obv. II 6 ff. contains a message of his to Dubuḫu-Ada, the son of Ibbi-Zikir: "*en-ma Š. si-in D.*"

For the name *Ša-nu*-NI-*um* (obv. III 3), cfr. *Ša-nu*-NI-*a*, *ARET* IV 1 (56); VIII 526 (28), (32). For me-te (te:me) (obv. II 2) the lexical lists have the following equivalences: *ra-ma-núm* / *ra-ma-nu-um*, cfr. Akkadian *rāmanu* "self." In the delivery-lists it refers to a person himself.[57] See for example TM.75.G.1587 rev. VII 8-14: "30+5 garments, those for I. himself (lú te:me *Ib*-NE-*um*), 150 garments, those for his farmer(s) (*ša-ti* engar-*sù*)," VIII 4-10: (1 garment) *ša-ti* te:me *En*-ḪAR-*ga-ma-al*$_6$ (50 garments) *ša-ti* engar-*sù*, VIII 11-IX 2: (1 garment) *ša-ti* te:me *Ib-da-ud* (37 garments) *ša-ti* engar-*sù*, IX 3-9: (1 garment) *ša-ti* te:me *Kam*$_4$-ʾà-LUM (44 garments) *ša-ti* engar-*sù* (parallel is TM.75.G.1864 rev. V 6-VII 7). Here, in obv. II 2, me-te could refer to Šema-Kura himself.

A-mùnu is a product obtained by adding water to malt. In Babylonia "dieses 'Malzwasser' ist auch ein Heilmittel in der Apotheke."[58] The problem is to determine the function of GIŠ-. The bilingual lexical lists have GIŠ-a-mùnu-ḪÚB (A, C, D), GIŠ-a-mùnu-mùnu-NU-ḪÚB (B). Only C has an Eblaite gloss: *mar-da*-LUM, perhaps a product which recalls làl mar-da-nu = *mar-da-[nu]*, in a late Akkadian list, see *AHw*, p. 610 "(ein Brei?);" *CAD* M I, p. 277 "(a variety of honey)." But the lexical lists also have: GIŠ-mùnu = *ḫi-ma-šum* / *ḫi-ma-su-um*, which is "an implement used in some operation performed on grain," according to M. Civil, because of the root *ḫmš*, (cfr. Akkadian *ḫamāšu*, *AHw*, p. 315: "abknicken;" *CAD* Ḫ, pp. 60-61: "(it) indicates a process performed on barley seeds").[59] In Fara, WF 106 is closed by the colophon: 67 lú GIŠ-mùnu(DIM_4), that is, people who can process malt.[60] An instrument related to GIŠ-a-mùnu is perhaps: a-mùnu-mùnu-ḪÚB-URUDU, in the unilingual list MEE III 45-46 (TM.75.G.1822+2551+) rev. III 4, duplicate TM.75.G.10011 + rev. III 4. SF 20 obv. VII 12-13 has: mùnu-mùnu-MUŠEN-URUDU, mùnu-mùnu-gan-MUŠEN-URUDU.[61]

The action expressed by sur refers to GIŠ-a-mùnu: "to process (the G.) well; this is the responsibility of those (who have received it)" (rev. I 1-3); sur is Akkadian *ṣaḫātu* "to extract sesame oil, to process wine and juices," *CAD* Ṣ, p. 60. GIŠ-geštin-sur-ra means

[57] See G. Pettinato, *MEE* II 37 rev. VIII 12, and the commentary at p. 258. For me-te, see B. Alster, *JCS* 26 (1974), pp. 178-180.

[58] M. Stol, *RlA* 7 (1987-1990), p. 328b.

[59] In *BaE*, p. 94.

[60] Cfr. P. Charvát, in K. Hecker - W. Sommerfeld, *Keilschriftliche Literaturen*, Berlin 1986, pp. 47-48. F. Pomponio, *SEL* 3 (1986), p. 15.

[61] Cfr. also Civil, *Ebla 1975-1985*, p. 155.

"drawn wine (*karānu ṣaḫtu*)," *CAD* Ṣ, p. 63-64.[62] Perhaps GIŠ-a-mùnu is the sprouted barley which one has to dry in order to stop the growth of the sprout.

5. Wine at Ebla[63]

Ebla itself produced wine. Lists of the assignment of fields show that some plots were planted with olives, GIŠ-ì-giš, and other smaller ones with vines, GIŠ-geštin.[64] The majority of the wine consumed in the city probably came from these vineyards, and documents numbers 3 and 4 published here probably refer to this production.

Other wine was given by some outlying towns, or by independent cities. Only one delivery, however, is noteworthy: 90 vessels, dug, from the city of Kakmium for the king and his vizier Ibbi-Zikir, TM.75.G.10191 obv. V 11-15. Generally, they were shipments in the sphere of exchanges of ceremonial goods, whose quantities are not specified but which, however, probably were of the type of those recorded here in texts numbers 3 and 4, that is, one or two jars, each one containing about 20 liters, and hence small quantities.

The independent city-states that furnished wine (5.2) were all located in the vicinity of Ebla: Kakmium, Manuwad, Ursaum (North), Burman, Dub (East, North-East), Ibubu, Imar (East), Garmeum, Gudadanum, Ibal (South-East), Utig.

5.1 Officials "in charge of wine," lú geštin[65]

"*Bu*"(MUNU$_3$)-[*ma-*]*il* lú geštin: *ARET* III 538 obv. I

En-na-NI lú geštin: TM.75.G.1379 rev. XI 1-2 (age of ArruLUM): 2593 rev. VIII 3-4.[66]
En-na-NI maškim *Ìr-ra-sá-mu* lú geštin: TM.75.G.1381 obv. VIII 12-13

[62] W. Farber, *Beschwörungsrituale an Ištar und Dumuzi*, Wiesbaden 1977, p. 88, writes: "Man könnte ausser der Bedeutung '(frisch) gepresster Wein/Traubensaft' jedoch auch—und gerade beim Gerbeprozess—an entwässerten und dadurch 'eingedickten' Saft denken." sur-ra is said also of beer: "drawn beer," according to A. Alberti - F. Pomponio, *Pre-Sargonic and Sargonic Texts from Ur Edited in UET 2, Supplement*, Rome 1986, p. 115, who quote *MAD* I: 129 obv. 2'-3', where kaš-su-ra precedes kaš-ús-sa "second-class beer."

[63] The following lists are based, beside the published texts, on a reading of the tablets TM.75.G.1216-2663, 10000-10281, and part of the other epigraphic material.

[64] Cfr. Archi, *Mélanges P. Garelli*, Paris 1991, pp. 212-214. The passage *ARET* VII 154 obv. III 5-9: 150 GÁNA-ki *wa* dug geštin GN PN, seems to mean that in this case someone received in addition to a field also an undetermined production of wine from that village.

[65] Further, see the obscure passage TM.75.G.2489 rev. V 2-10; 1 túg-NI.NI *Ra*-PÉŠ-*tum* DU.DU *si-in Du-ub*^{ki} dub-zu-zu kin$_x$-ak *ḫa-ri* lú geštin.

[66] 2593 rev. VIII 2-10: 1+1+1 garments 1 dumu-nita ur$_x$ lú geštin *wa* 1 dumu-nita *En-na*-NI lú geštin *in Da-na*[- šu-ba$_4$-ti].

En-na-[d]*Ra-sa-ap* lú geštin: *ARET* X 61 obv. I 4-5; 64 obv. I 5-6; 65 obv. I 4-5. *En-na-*[d]*Ra-sa-ap* lú geštin lú *I-bi-zi-kir*: *ARET* VIII 525 (45)

Ìr-ra-sá-mu(?), see sub *En-na-NI*

[d]*Ku-ra-ma-i-da* lú geštin: *ARET* IV 7 (13)

Ma-ga-da lú geštin: 75.G.2240 obv. VIII 17-18 (*M.* lú geštin maškim *I-da-ni-ki-mu in Da-na-ne*[ki] šu-ba_4-ti); 2243 rev. III 3-4

NI-*ba*-NI lú geštin: *ARET* VIII 542 (17); TM.75.G.2402 obv. VII 6-7 (13 muḫaldim *wa* NI-*ba*-NI lú geštin)

Zi-la-BE lú geštin: *ARET* X 65 rev. IV 14-V 1.

5.2 Towns delivering wine

Scheme: "1(+1+1) article of clothing for (PN of) GN who has delivered (šu-mu-"$taka_4$" = š.m.t.) wine / new wine (geštin-gibil)." The names of the people who have delivered and brought the wine are in brackets. For other kinds of deliveries the full passage is given.

A-ba-um[ki]: TM.75.G.2490 rev. IV 14 (1+1 garments *Iš-má-da-mu A.* š.-m.-t. geštin *I-bí-zi-kir in Mar-tu*[ki] šu-ba_4-ti)

A-ba-zu-nu[ki]: *ARET* III 595 III; TM.75.G.2468 obv. VI 10

Ar-u_9*-gú*[ki]: *ARET* III 538 rev. III ([...]dam *A.* š.m.t. geštin *Ib-rí-um*)

Bur-ma-an[ki]: TM.75.G.1523 obv. II 13 (*Ib-dur-i-šar*; geštin *Ib-rí-um*)

ARET III 119 II ([...] *B.* ḫi-mu-DU 1 gu_4 udu-udu geštin ama-gal en):

Du-ub[ki]: *ARET* I 14 (16) (*Zi-zu*); 17 (51) (*Iš*$_{11}$*-a-ma-lik*); II 14 (34); III 58 II; 196 II (*A-mu-ra*); IV 10 (45) (*Zi-zu*); 19 (13) (*Ìr-am*$_6$*-ma-lik*); TM.75.G.1326 obv. IV 5; 1329 obv. X 10; 1337 rev. IV 6 and VII 5 (ʾ*À-zi-gú*); 1344 obv. IV 8 (*Iš-ma-aḫ-ma-lik* šeš en *D.*; geštin-geštin), rev. VII 3 (*Ìr-am*$_6$*-ma-lik*; geštin-geštin); 1418 obv. I 4; 1457 obv. IV 9 (š.m.t. geštin en); 1786 obv. III 10 (*A-mu-ra*); 1884 rev. III 15 (*Ìr-am*$_6$*-ma-lik*); 2400 rev. I 2 (*Ìr-am*$_6$*-ma-lik*); 2526 obv. IV 15 (*Ìr-am*$_6$*-ma-lik*; *in Dur*-NE-*du*[ki] šu-ba_4-ti); 10082 obv. VII 13 (geštin *I-bí-zi-kir*); 10135 obv. X 3 (*A-mu-ru*$_{12}$); 10150 obv. IV 3 (*Ìr-am*$_6$*-da-ar*)

2632 obv. VI 5 (1[+1+1 garments] *Ìr-am*$_6$*-ma-lik D.* ḫi-mu-DU geštin)

INDICES

1) Personal names

A-bu	3 obv. II 5, rev. II 2 (lú *Du-na-ù*), 10, V 6; 4 obv. III 2, 9, IV 3, rev. I 9, V 6
A-bù	4 obv. IV 6
A-bù-^{d}*Ku-ra*	3 rev. V 1
ᵓ*À-da-ša*	3 obv. I 5 (*'À. Ù-kul*^{ki}), V 2 (*'À.* lú *Na-mi*), rev. I 4(?), II 8
*A-*ḪAR*-ar-mu*	3 obv. I 4, V 1, rev. III 2, IV 7, V 8
*A-*NE*-*ᵓ*à*	3 obv. III 5 (*Ar-šè-a-ḫu* lú *A.*), 8 (*Bù-da-*NI lú *A.*), rev. II 16, IV 5, V 4
*A-*NE-⌈u_9⌉	3 obv. III 2 ([x-*d*]*a*-[N]I lú *A.*)
A-⌈x⌉-⌈x⌉-⌈x⌉-⌈x⌉	3 rev. III 9
Ar-šè-a-ḫu	3 obv. III 4 (*A.* lú *A-*NE*-'à*)
Ba-aš-dar	2 rev. IV 6
Bar-za-ma-ù	3 obv. II 1, rev. III 14
Bù-[	3 obv. VII 10
*Bù-da-*NI	3 obv. III 7 (*B.* lú *A-*NE*-*ᵓ*à*)
Bù-la	3 obv. IV 7, V 17
Bù-ma-ù	2 rev. I 2, III 2
Da-kùn-da-mu	4 obv. IV 8
Du-bí-ga-lu	2 obv. I 4
Du-bí-zi-kir	3 obv. VII 4(?)
Du-bù-ḫu-^{d}ᵓ*À-da*	4 obv. II 7
Du-na-ù	3 obv. II 12, rev. II 3
*Du-*NE*-a-*NE	3 obv. V 12, VI 4, 9, rev. VI 17, VII 4
Gi-la-a-ḫu	5 obv. II 6
Gi-rí	3 obv. I 9, VI 12, VII 3, 13
I-bí-zi-kir	1 obv. II 1, rev. I 4; 2 obv. VI 1, rev. III 6; 3 rev. IV 1; 4 obv. IV 11 (*Da-ra-um*^{ki}), rev. I 6
I-da-ne-ki-mu	2 obv. I 2, II 3; 3 obv. I 2, IV 5, 11, 14, V 9, 15, VI 7
In-ti	5 obv. I 4
Ìr$^{!}$*-za-*NI	5 obv. III 1
Iš$_{11}$*-m*[*a-ì/lik*]	4 rev. II 3
*I-ti-*NI	3 rev. I 2, II 3, VI 7
*I-ti-*LUM	5 obv. II 4
Na-mi	3 obv. V 3 (ᵓ*À-da-ša* lú *N.*)
NI*-a-*LUM	3 rev. III 4 (I dug lú PN PN_2 N. mu-DU); IV 2 (1 dug geštin lú PN PN_2 N. mu-DU), V 2 (] PN N.). [NI*-a-lu*, var. NI*-a-ru*$_{12}$ is

	a PN, see *ARES* I, 269 (ugula bìr-BAR.AN IGI.NITA), and 75.1669 rev. VII 7, *SEb* 2, 14 (a man from Karkemish)
NI-*da-ni*	5 obv. III 5
NI-PI-NI-LUM	3 rev. II 11
Puzur$_4$*-ra*-BE	3 obv. IV 2, rev. III 3; 5 obv. I 2
Puzur$_4$*-ra-ma-lik*	3 obv. III 10
Sa-lu-du	4 rev. II 5
Sá-mu	3 obv. III 12, rev. VII 3
Ša-nu-NI-*um*	5 obv. III 3
Ša-⸢x⸣[-	3 rev. VI 16
Šè-ma-^{d}*Ku-ra*	5 rev. III 1
Šu-NI-*lum*	3 obv. II 10
T[*i*-(x-)]*m*[*a*(-x)]	3 obv. VII 9
U[R-	3 obv. VII 6
Ù-ti	2 rev. V 3
Za-a-šè	4 obv. II 11
[x-*d*]*a*-[N]I	3 obv. III 1 ([x.] lú *A*-NE-⸢*u*$_9$⸣
[x-N]I$^?$-LUM	3 obv. II 14
[x-]*si*$^?$*-mi*[- -LU]M	3 rev. V 13

2) Geographical names

Ad-da-ti-gú<ki>	4 obv. III 3, rev. I 7
Da-ra-um^{ki}	4 obv. IV 12
Ib-su^{ki}	3 rev. VI 4
Ì-mar^{ki}	3 obv. II 8, rev. V 11
Kam$_4$*-lu-lu*^{ki}	2 rev. IV 9; 4 obv. V 4 (simug-simug *K.*), 8 (nagar-nagar *K.*)
Lu-ba-an^{ki}	3 rev. II 6
Mu-ru$_{12}$^{ki}	4 obv. III 8
Na-gàr^{ki}	4 obv. I 3, II 1 (en)
Si-si^{ki}	2 rev. II 4
Ši-sal^{ki}	3 obv. IV 9, V 5, VI 2
Ù-kul^{ki}	3 obv. I 7

3) Glossary

AN.ŠÈ.GÚ "total"	4 rev. V 1
áb-peš (peš:áb) "young cow"	2 obv. IV 1
al$_6$ "upon"	5 rev. I 3
áš-da "from"	3 obv. VI 14
ba-rúm	2 rev. IV 4
dam dingir "priestess"	4 rev. II 6
dingir "god"	4 obv. II 12 (lú dingir[-dingir])

dub "document"	1 rev. III 4
dug "jar"	3 obv. I 1, *passim*; 4 obv. I 1, *passim*
dumu-mí "daughter"	4 obv. II 6, rev. II 2
dumu-nita "son"	1 obv. II 4 (3 d.), rev. II 5 (3 d., 5 rev. I 4 (3 d.)
é "house"	3 obv. V 11 and VI 13 (é en), rev. III 11, IV 8, VI 8 (é en); 4 obv. II 4, V 2 (simug-simug), 6 (é nagar-nagar)
è "issue"	4 rev. V 2
edin "plain"	2 obv. IV 1
en "king"	1 obv. I 2, II 3, III 3, rev. I 2, II 4, III 3; 2 obv. IV 3, rev. I 4, III 8; 3 obv. II 7 (en *Ì-mar*^{ki}), VI 13 (é en), rev. III 10, V 10 (en *Ì-mar*^{ki}), VI 8 (é en); 4 obv. I 9 (en *Na-gàr*^{ki}), II 13(?)
GÁNA-ki (a field measure)	1 obv. III 2; 2 obv. I 1, 3 rev. I 1
geštin "wine"	3 obv. I 1, *passim*; 4 obv. I 1, *passim*
gi-li "custody"	2 rev. III 4
GIŠ-a-mùnu "damp malt"	5 obv. I 1, *passim*
GIŠ-ir:nun "scented wood of cedar"	2 rev. V 7
GIŠ-taškarin "boxwood"	2 rev. V 6
gú-bar (a measure for grain)	1 obv. I 1; 2 obv. II 1, 2, rev. I 3, II 2
gu_4 "ox"	2 obv. III 1
gu_4-maḫ "adult cow"	1 rev. II 1 (maḫ:gu_4); 2 rev. III 1
gu_4-tur "calf"	1 rev. II 2
ì-na-sum "to give"	3 obv. VII 11
ì-ti "he was (present)"	3 rev. VI 5; 4 obv. III 4, IV 10, rev. I 5
ib (an official)	4 obv. II 3 (ib-ib)
in "in"	2 rev. III 3; 3 obv. IV 4, 10, 13, 16, V 8, 14, VI 6, 10, VII 2, 12, rev. II 7, III 11, VI 3; 4 obv. I 7, II 8
ir-mu (IX month)	1 rev. III 5
iti "month"	1 rev. III 5
ká "gate; administrative section"	2 rev. II 3
kú "to eat; meal"	3 obv. VI 15, rev. III 12, IV 10(?)
kù-bar_6 "silver"	2 obv. III 2, rev. IV 5, 7, V 1, 4
kù-gi "gold"	2 obv. III 3, rev. IV 2
lá "subtract, less"	2 obv. III 2, 3 rev. VII 6
li(*-im*) "thousand"	1 obv. I 1, *passim*
lú "that (of)"	1 obv. III 3, *passim*

ma-ḫu-at / ma-i-at "hundred thousand"[73]	1 obv. I 1 (*ma-ḫu-at*); 2 obv. 1 and 5 (*ma-i-at*), rev. I 3 (*ma-ḫu-at*), II 2 (*ma-i-at*)
ma-lik-tum "queen"	3 obv. V 7
ma-na "mina"	2 obv. III 2, 3, rev. IV 2, 5, 7, V 1, 4
me-te(te:me) "self"	5 obv. II 2
mi(*-at*) "hundred"	1 obv. I 1, *passim*
MU	3 obv. III 13
mu-DU "delivery"	3 obv. VI 16, rev. III 5, IV 3
nag "to drink"	3 obv. IV 3, VI 5, rev. VI 1
nagar "carpenter"	4 obv. V 7 (é nagar-nagar *Kam*$_4$*-lu-lu*^{ki})
níg-gul:é "free present, good at disposal"	1 obv. II 5, rev. II 6 (see nu-nig-gul:é)
NÍG-M[I]$^?$-⌈x⌉	3 rev. II 13
níg-mu-sá "marriage"	4 obv. I 8(?)
níg-sa$_{10}$ (NÍNDA×ŠE.ZA) "price, value"	2 obv. III 4, rev. IV 3, V 5
níg-šè-nu-šè "package"	4 obv. I 2
nu-níg-gul:é "not at disposal"	1 obv. III 1, rev. III 2
nu-zé "not to be drawn"	1 obv. II 6, rev. III 1 (nu-zé-*su-ma*)
rí-pap "ten thousand"	1 obv. I 1, III 2, rev. I 1; 2 obv. I 1, II 1, 2, IV 2, rev. I 1, II 2, III 7
sa$_6$ "good"	5 rev. I 2
sig$_{15}$ (a cereal)	2 obv. II 2
si-in "for"	3 obv. IV 8, V 4, VI 1, rev. II 5, 12; 4 obv. III 7
simug "smith"	4 obv. V 3 (é simug-simug *Kam*$_4$*-lu-lu*^{ki})
-sù "his, its"	2 obv. III 2; 5 rev. I 3
-su-ma "their (dual)"	1 obv. II 2, rev. II 3, III 1
sur "to press"	5 rev. I 1
še "barley"	1 obv. I 1; 2 obv. II 1, rev. I 3, II 2
še-SAG×ḪA-mul "debt with interest"	2 rev. IV 8, V 2
šu-ba$_4$-ti "to receive"	3 obv. V 13, rev. VII 1, 5

[73] The two writings alternate in document 2, and the bilingual lexical list A$_2$ has both *ma-i-at* and *ma-i-ḫu-at*. That *ma-*(*i-*)*ḫu-at* also means "hundred thousand" is demonstrated by the mathematical tablet TM.75.G.1392 where 2 *ma-i-ḫu*<*-at*> 6 *rí-pap* is the sum of adding 2 *ma-i-at* and 6 *rí-pap*. The most recent edition of the tablet is that of Archi, *RA* 83 (1989), pp. 2-5. While *ma-i-at* is /majjat/ "very much," it is not easy to provide a convincing interpretation for *ma-*(*i-*)*ḫu-at*, see M. Krebernik, *ZA* 73 (1983), p. 44.

SOURCES AND MONOGRAPHS ON THE ANCIENT NEAR EAST

Editors: Giorgio Buccellati, Marilyn Kelly-Buccellati

These two series make available original documents in English translation (Sources) and important studies by modern scholars (Monographs) as a contribution to the study of the history, religion, literature, art, and archaeology of the Ancient Near East. Inexpensive and flexible in format, they are meant to serve the specialist by bringing within easy reach basic publications, often in updated versions, to provide imaginative education outlets for undergraduate and graduate courses, and to reach interested segments of the educated lay audience.

SANE 1/1

The Akkadian Namburbi Texts: An Introduction, by Richard I. Caplice

Namburbi is the title of a group of typical Babylonian incantations, used to "undo" or avert portended evil. Consisting of both rituals and prayers, they provide a response to the observed events taken by the Mesopotamians to be signs of future happenings; thus they are the practical correlate of the "omen texts," which list such portents and their significance. The fascicle by Caplice includes a long introduction, which explains the nature of the texts and their ritual *Sitz im Leben*, and the translation, with notes, of 14 representative texts, ranging from a Ritual for the Evil of a Snake to a Ritual to Secure Brisk Trade.

Second printing, with minor correction, 1982

Library of Congress Card Number: 74-78770
ISBN: 0-89003-003-0

PREFACE

Like other types of ritual text preserved in cuneiform documents, the namburbi texts offer us a fascinating yet tantalizing insight into man's religious and cosmological conceptions at an earlier stage of civilization: fascinating in what they reveal, yet tantalizing because the accidents of time have left us only remnants and hints of a past era. Those texts that have been preserved to us are often broken or abraded or difficult of interpretation, and even when fully preserved they require an unusual measure of perception and open-mindedness if we are to see them as integral parts of their own culture.

This monograph is a small attempt to bridge the gap that separates us from these texts. An introductory section sketches the character, contents, and significance of the texts. In the space available, the sketch is necessarily summary; an attempt has been made to face the main issues posed by the texts, and to give some bibliographical indications for the reader who wishes to investigate further, but neither full analysis nor complete documentation is attempted.

The second section presents fourteen namburbi texts in translation. The dominant criteria for their selection have been representativeness, relative completeness of preservation, and non-availability hitherto in English translation. The translations offered proceed, in general, from simple rituals to more complex ones. The translation is generally *ad litteram*, but the presentation has in other respects been simplified: indentation replaces the ancient use of dividing lines to form "paragraphs" on the tablet, and line division is indicated only for the line at the beginning of each paragraph by the pertinent line number. The sigla used include square brackets [ ], which enclose destroyed and hypothetically restored sections of the text; round brackets ( ), which enclose phrases implied but not expressed by the text; pointed brackets < >, which enclose words or signs judged to be mistakenly omitted by the ancient scribe.

B. TEXTS IN TRANSLATION

Text 1. Ritual for the evil of a snake

1. – If in the beginning of the year on the first day of Nisan, or on the first day of Ayar, a snake is seen either in daytime or at night, that man (who saw it) will die during that year. If that man is desirous of life, he gashes(?)[1] (his) head (and) shaves his cheeks. For those three months he will be sore beset, but he will get well.

Reference. *CT* 38 33:1.
Notes. [1]See *AHw ḫarāru(m)* I, *CAD ḫarāru* B.

Text 2. Ritual for the evil of luminous flashes

1. – Namburbi to dissipate the evil of flashing light. [You throw] tamarisk, *mashtakal*-plant, "pure-plant," datewood, apple-wood, fig-wood (and) fir-wood into well water, (and) set them overnight under the stars. In the morning you wash (the threatened man?) with water. You mix beer, *kalû*-clay, *kalguqqu*-clay (and) algae in myrtle oil. You a[noint him and] dress him in a clean garment. You show [him] silver and gold, [and the evil] of flashing light will not approach the man.

Colophon (Exemplar A).–Tablet 20 of *Šumma ālu ina mēlê šakin* ("If a city is set on a height"). (Catchline:) If a dead person appears like a living one in a man's house, that man will die, (there will be) destruction of the house. Written according to its original (and) [collated].

Reference. *Or* 40 (1971) 165f.

Text 3. Ritual for the evil of a bow[1]

1. – Namburbi [to dissipate] the evil of every kind of bow, that it may not approach.

3. – [Its ritual]: you set out [an offering arrangement for] Ea and Ishtar. You sacrifice [a kid befo]re the Bowstar. [You pou]r out [a censer of juniper and fine flour]. You express greeting[2] to Marduk. You present to [Nin-ild]u [a bronze axe and a saw]. You recite before Ishtar [the incantation "You are merciful, . . . you are life-g]iving."

8. – You set out [. . . before Ea, Asalluhi] and Shamash. You sacrifice[3] [. . . on] the river bank.

Reference. *Or* 39 (1970) 116f.

Notes. [1]The text is a brief version of *LKA* 113; restorations are drawn from the latter.
[2]*takarrab.*
[3]Or: perform (*teppuš*).

Text 4. Ritual for the evil of ants

1. – Namburbi for the evil of ants which have been seen in a man's house, that its (the portent's) evil may not approach the man and his house. Its ritual[1]: you sprinkle sweet-smelling oil over the ants and their nest. You bury gypsum (and) horned alkali in their tunnel. You mix dust from a ship, clay[2] from a river meadow (and) dust from the threshold of[3] an outer gate either in well water or in river water, and you sprinkle (this mixture over the nest). You set censers of juniper and myrrh at both thresholds. Then its evil will be dissipated.

Colophon (Exemplar A).–(Catchline:) If moths are seen in a man's house, the owner of that house will become important. Tablet 35 of *Šumma ālu ina melê šakin.* Written according to a (wooden) tablet of Akkad (that is, Babylonia), an original of Babylon; checked (and) collated. Tablet of Nabû-aḫa-iddina, scribe, son of Nabû-šuma-[ib]ni, scribe of (the city) Assur.

Colophon (Exemplar B). – Written according to its original (and) col[lated]. Tablet of Nabû-šuma-iškun, son of Kandalānu.

References. *KAR* 377 rev. 37-40; *STT* 242 rev. 19-23.
Notes. [1]" Its ritual" is omitted in the *KAR* exemplar (= A).
[2]For "clay" the *STT* exemplar (= B) has "dust."
[3]B omits "the threshold of."

Text 5. Ritual for the evil of a frog

1. – Namburbi for the evil of a frog, [to avert its evil], that it may not [approach] the man and his house.

3. – Its [ritual: you make two images of the frog(?), on]e of silver, [one of gold(?)]. You [go(?)] upon a river bank. [You set out] an offering arrangement before [Ea]. You offer sacrifices. [You serve] the shoulder portion (and) intestines. [You pour out] dates (and) fine flour. [You set out] confections of [honey (and) ghee]. You set out a censer of juniper. [You recite as follows].

9. – Incantation: Enki, king of the *Apsû* . . . .[1]

Colophon. – [. . . written] according to [its original]; checked (and) collated. [. . . Tablet of] Kiṣir-Nabû [who tru]sts [in Nab]û and Tašmētu, [son of] Šamaš-ibni, incantation priest of the temple of (the god) [Aššur], [son of Nabû]-besun, incantation priest [of the temple of Aššur]. It was [hastily] excerpted.

Reference. *LKA* 118.
Notes. [1]Only fragments of the remainder of this Sumerian prayer and of further ritual directions are preserved.

Text 6. Ritual for the evil of a monstrous birth

1. – If there was a misformed newborn creature in a man's house–whether (born) of cattle, sheep, ox, [goat], horse, dog, pig, or human being–in order to avert that evil, [that it may not approach] the man and his house (you perform the following ritual).

6. – You go to the river and construct a reed hut. [You scatter] garden plants. You set up a reed altar. Upon the reed altar you pour out seven food offerings, beer, dates, (and) fine flour. [You set out] a censer of juniper. You fill three bowls with fine beer, and [you set out] loaves of . . .-bread, DÌM-bread (and) "ear-shaped" bread (along with) one grain of silver (and) one grain of gold. You place a gold . . . on the head of that misborn creature. You attach a gold breastplate to red thread. You bind it on his breast. You cast that misborn creature on garden plants. You have that man kneel and recite as follows.

15. – Incantation: Shamash, judge of heaven and earth, lord of justice and equity, director of upper and lower regions! Shamash, it is in your power to bring the dead to life, to release the captive. Shamash, I have approached you! Shamash, I have sought you out! Shamash, I have turned to you! Avert from me the evil of this misborn creature! May it not affect me! May its evil be far from my person, that I may daily bless you (and) those who see me may forever [sing] your praise!

23. – You have him recite [this] incantation three times. The man's house [will then be at peace] . . . . Before the river [you recite] as follows.

Rev. 1. – [Incantation: y]ou, River, are the creator of everything. . . .-sun, the son of Zerûti, whose [personal god is Nabû, whose personal goddess] is Tashmētu, who [is beset by] an evil misborn creature, is therefore frightened (and) terrified. Avert from him the evil of this misborn creature! May the evil not approach, may it not draw near, [may it not press upon him]! May that evil go out from his person, that he may daily bless you (and) those who see [him] may forever sing your praise! By the command of Ea and Asalluhi, remove that evil! May your banks not release it! Take it down to your depths! Extract that evil! Give happiness (and) health![1]

Rev. 13. – You recite this three times, and purify the man with water. You throw tamarisk, Dilbat-plant, *shalālu*-reed, a date-palm shoot, (and) the misborn creature, together with its provisions and its gifts, into the river, and you undo the offering arrangement and prostrate yourself. That man goes to his house.

Rev. 17. – [You string] carnelian, lapis lazuli, serpentine, *pappardillu*-stone, *papparminû*-stone, bright obsidian, *hilibû*-stone, [TUR_7.MI.NA-stone], (and) breccia on a necklace. You place it around his neck for seven days . . . . The evil of that misborn creature will be dissipated.

Colophon (Exemplar A).– [Exerpted] for perfor[mance] . . . .

Colophon (Exemplar B). – [Written acc]ording to a (wooden) [tablet].

Colophon (Exemplar C). – (Traces of the colophon are preserved).

Reference. *Or* 34 (1965) 125-130.

Notes. [1]In the translation of *Or* 34, p. 129, the line which serves as a marker of paragraph division should be after line 12, not before it.

Text 7. Ritual for the evil of a dog[1]

1. – [Namburbi] for the evil of a dog [which howls and moans in a man's house, that the evil of th]at dog [may not approach the man and his house].

3. – You make a clay image of a dog. Before [Shamash] you recite an incantation three times. You go to the river and immerse yourself, [seven times facing upstream, seven times] facing downstream. [The evil of]

that dog will not approach the man and his house. Incantation: Enki, king of the *Apsû,* king of Eridu are you. May the evil portent of the dog which confronts you not come near him! May it not beset him! [End formula of the incantation].

10. – Namburbi for the evil of a dog which howls (and) moans in a man's house, or spatters its urine upon a man. Three times you recite (the incantation), then the evil of that dog will not approach the man and his house.

14. – Its ritual: you make a clay image of a dog. You place cedar wood upon its neck. You sprinkle oil upon its head. You clothe it in goat's hair. You set horse bristles in its tail. At the river bank you set up a reed altar before Shamash. You arrange twelve emmer loaves. You heap up dates and fine flour. You set out confections of honey and ghee. You set up a jug, (and) fill two bottles with fine beer and set them out. You set out a censer of juniper. You libate fine beer. You have that man kneel and raise that figurine, and he recites as follows.

24. – Incantation: Shamash, king of heaven (and) earth, judge of the upper and lower regions, light of the gods, governor of mankind, pronouncer of judgement on the great gods, I turn to you, seek you out. Among the gods, command that I live! May the gods who are with you command my prosperity! Because of this dog, which has voided its urine upon me, I am frightened, alarmed, and terrified. Avert from me the evil of this dog, that I may sing your praise!

34. – When he has recited this[2] before Shamash, you recite as follows over that figurine.

36. – I have given you as a [replacemen]t for myself, I have given you as a substitute for myself. [I have stripped off all the evil] of my body upon you. I have stripped off, I have stripped off all the evil of my flesh upon you. I have stripped off all the evil of my figure upon you. I have stripped off all the evil before me and behind me upon you.

Rev. 4. – When you have recited this, you leave the presence of Shamash, and you go off to the river, and recite as follows.

Rev. 6. – Incantation: you, River, are the creator of everything. I, so-and-so, the son of so-and-so, whose personal god is so-and-so, whose personal goddess is so-and-so, have been spattered with this dog's urine, so that I am frightened and afraid. [Just as] this figurine will not return to its place, may its evil not approach! May it not come near! May it not press upon me! May it not affect me! May the evil of that dog be far from my person, that I may daily bless you, that those who see me may forever sing your [praise]! Incantation: take that dog straight down to your depths! Do not release it! Take it down to your depths! Extract the evil of that dog from my body! Grant me happiness and health!

Rev. 19. – When you have recited this three times, you throw that dog into the river, and that man does not look behind him. He enters a tavern, and [its] e[vil will be dissipated].

Colophon (Exemplar A). – (Catchline:) For the evil of a badger which is in a man's meadow. Written according to its original (and) col[lated]. Tablet of Nabû-besunu, incantation priest of the temple of Aššur, offspring of Baba-[šuma]-ibni, the high official of Ešarra. Who takes this tablet, may Šamaš take away his eye(sight).

Colophon (Exemplar C). – Written according to its original (and) collated. Written by Mušallim-Baba, young apprentice scribe. Tablet of Qurdi-Nergal, priest of Zababa and Baba, (the gods who reside) in Kapar-ilāni(?) (and) in Harran and Huzirna.

Reference. *Or* 36 (1967) 1-8.

Notes. [1]This is the first of our translations to exemplify a tablet containing more than one ritual. While rituals so combined on a single tablet can be responses to quite diverse portents, the present text gives two rites for the evil of a dog: the first (lines 1-9) is composed of the preparation of a clay image, immersion in the river, an unspecified prayer to Shamash, and a brief invocation of Enki, and it contains the usual final formula of a ritual, "The evil . . . will not approach." Neither the use of the image nor the prayer to Shamash are specifically indicated; these were either left to the discretion of the liturgist, or considered to be supplied by the parallel portions of the second ritual. The second ritual (lines 10-end) has a more complex series of ritual directions, and includes prayers to Shamash and to the divinized River.

[2]One variant adds: "three times."

Text 8. Prayer for the evil of a snake

1. – Incantation: Ea, Shamash and Asalluhi, great gods who hand down the verdicts of heaven and earth, who determine the fates, who make cult-cities great, who lay the foundation of throne daises, who confirm the lots, who fashion the designs, who apportion the lots, who make sanctuaries stable, who purify rituals, who know the purification ceremony–the determination of fates (and) the fashioning of designs are in your hands. The fates of life you alone determine. [The designs] of life you alone fashion. [The decisions] of life you alone make. You inspect all throne daises of god and [goddess]. You alone are the great gods who direct the decisions of heaven and earth, the depth of the seas. Your word is life, your utterance is well-being, your pronouncement is life itself. You alone tread in the midst of the distant heavens: you who do away with evil, who establish the good, who undo evil signs (and) portents, frightful (and) evil dreams, who cut the thread of evil.

19. – I, whose [mouth] is pure, who know the pure rites of <the *Apsû*>, have poured out water (and) cleansed the ground for you. Pure chairs I have set forth for you to sit upon. Pure red garments I have presented to you. An offering arrangement I have set out for you. A pure libation I have poured out for you. A libation bowl with *nashpu*-beer I have set up for you. Wine and beer I have poured out for you. Because the rites of the great gods are (now) perfected [and] because the success of rituals rests with you, on this day stand by this sleeping person[1] [who] stands before you! . . . Greatly determine (this) fate: that he may (again) eat with his mouth, that he may hear with his ears. May this [man] be bright as the [heavens], may he be [pure] as the earth, may he shine like the midst of heaven! Let the tongue of evil stand aside![2] I, so-and-so, son of [so-and-so], your servant, am afraid, frightened and terrified.

33b. – For the evil of a snake.[3]

Reference. *Iraq* 18 (1956) pl. XIV.

Notes. [1]In place of *ṣa-al-[li]* "sleeper" read probably <*mu*>*-ṣa-al-[li]* "suppliant, one who is praying."

[2]This injunction for cultic silence has been discussed by Erica Reiner, *Studies in Honor of Benno Landsberger on his Seventy-fifth Birthday April 21, 1965* (*AS* 16, 1965) 247-251.

[3]As normally with cuneiform texts, the title is placed at the end as a subscript. On the tablet it appears on the same line as the end of the text of the prayer, without being set off by a dividing line: this procedure is unusual when compared with texts from the Aššurbanipal library.

Text 9. Ritual for the evil of fungus

23′. – [If] there is fungus in a man's house, on the outer north wall, the owner of the house will die and his [house] will be scattered. To avert the evil, you make six axes of tamarisk and scrape away some of the fungus with them. You sweep with a datepalm branch from the north (side of the tree). You gather (lit.: receive) it into a reed basket. You incense it with a torch and place mud and gypsum on it, and its evil will be dissipated. You recite "Ea performed (the incantation), Ea undid (the evil)." On that day the [own]er(?) of the house slaughters a red male sheep before Ishum, reciting "May Ishum receive this." You place the head and hocks in beer and bury them at the outer gate. You have that man stand over them. You throw holy water over him, and recite as follows.

34′. – *Enuru*-incantation:[1] pure river, clean river, water of the pure Tigris, the [clean(?)] river, joined with(?) (water from) the *Apsû*! Tigris, mother of the mountain land! May he be pure as heaven! May he be clean as earth! May he be bright as the midst of heaven! Let the evil tongue stand aside![2] Be conjured by heaven, be conjured by earth!

40′. – You throw that holy water over him, and its (the portent's) evil will be dissipated.

Colophon (Exemplar A). – Finished. (Catchline:) [If . . .] of the steppe are in a man's house, the owner of the house will die.

Colophon (Exemplar B). – Spell to avert (the evil portended by) fungus.

Colophon (Exemplar C). – (Catchline:) [If . . .] does not prick (its) ears(?). Copy of a (wooden) tablet of Akkad. Property of the palace.

Reference. *Or* 40 (1971) 141:23′-40′.

Notes. [1]This incantation is written entirely in Sumerian. The meaning of the Sumerian term *é-nu-ru* is unclear; see A. Falkenstein, *Die Haupttypen der sumerischen Beschwörung literarisch untersucht* (*LSS* NF 1, 1931) 5f.

[2]See text 8, note 2.

Text 10. Ritual for the evil of dust from a place of mourning[1]

1. – Namburbi for the evil of dust from a place of mourning, that its evil may not approach the man, that it may not overtake (him) or (effect) anything whatever. On a propitious day that man undergoes a cleansing rite (and) is "sanctified." He arranges a reed altar before Shamash. He libates offerings of *miḫḫu*-beer. He prostrates himself and kneels. You recite as follows: "I have turned to you, Shamash, because life is precious. May the evil of the dust I saw from a place of mourning be dissipated and dissolved!" Three times you recite this [before Shama]sh.

10. – Incantation: Shamash, you are judge of justice and equity, who sets right the wronged one and the beaten one, who drives away all the sorcery practiced against me, who undoes the sin of the wronged one, though it is unconscious, (who undoes) the fault (and) the crime blamed on me, though I am unaware of it. Shamash, avert from me the evil of the dust from a place of mourning which I placed on my head (or) my body! All unknowingly, I have been put at enmity with peer (and) companion, friend (and) associate, noble (and) prince. May I be clean as pure water, that I may publish your greatness, that I may sing your praise!

Rev. 8. – You go apart, and before Ea, [Shamash], and Asalluhi [you set out] an offering arrangement. You offer three sacrifices and that man [goes] to the river bank. He takes off his [garment] and before [Shamash] you sacrifice a sheep. For seven days he does not go forth from (his) door. Its evil will be dissipated.

Colophon. – Written according to its original (and) collated. Tablet of Kiṣir-<Aš>šur, incantation priest of the temple of Aššur, son of Nabû-besunu, incantation priest of the temple of <Aš>šur, son of Baba-šuma-iddina, incantation priest of the temple of <Aš>šur.

Reference. *LKA* 119.

Notes. [1]This text was edited by Ebeling, *RA* 48 (1954) 178-181.

Text 11. Ritual for the evil of a lizard

12′. – Namburbi for the evil of any lizard, that it (the evil) may not approach a man and his house. Let that man be "sanctified" on a propitious day. You sweep the roof. [You sprinkle] pure water. You set up a reed altar. You scatter dates (and) fine flour. [You set out] confections of honey (and) ghee. You offer sacrifices.[1] You set out a censer of juniper. You scatter *isqūqu*-flour. [You make a clay] image of the lizard. You draw a design on a large bowl. You place the clay image of the lizard upon (the design). You set (it) at the side of the offering arrangement. You have that man stand over tamarisk wood. You take his hand. Three times you have him recite the incantation "Shamash, great lord, judge of the Igigi."

19′. – Incantation: Shamash, great lord, judge of the Igigi and the Anunnaki,[2] director of the black-headed folk,[3] lord of the dead and the living are you. Exalted judge whose command cannot be changed, whose assent no god can alter, you are the lord. Your word is indeed great, your command cannot be for[gotten], your prayer cannot be rivalled, [your] command [is exalted] like (that of) Anu, your father. Your word is outstanding among the gods your brothers. Noble lord [whose power is fearful],[4] merciful god who rules all things, Shamash, as you come forth[5] [you see all people]. You direct the "cattle of Shakkan," the living creatures. Stand by me, [Shamash, hear my words]! Because of the evil of the portent of a lizard which took place in my house(!) (and) [confronted my] eyes, [I am] afraid, frightened (and) terrified. . . . [Avert (the evil) from me, that I may not] die, that I may not be wronged! [May its evil not approach me! May it cross the river! May it pass over the mountain]! May it be 3600 miles distant [from my person! May I, your servant, have health (and) well-b]eing, that [I may sing your praise]!

Reference. *STT* 63:12'-31'.

Notes. [1]The logogram used suggests animal sacrifices.

[2]For these designations of the gods see Burkhart Kienast, "*Igigū* und *Anunnakū* nach den akkadischen Quellen," *AS* 16, 141-158.

[3]A poetic expression for "mankind."

[4]This and the following lines are restored from the duplicate *Or* 34 (1965) 117:14' ff.; see also *BMS* 60 and *KAR* 246, and Ebeling's treatment of these two texts, *MVAG* 23 (1918) 40-43.

[5]A reference to the rising of the sun.

Text 12. Ritual for the evil of lizards

1. – (A line invoking Shamash) has been lost.[1] Powerful lord, scion of Eridu, wise one of the universe [are you (Marduk)]! Shamash and Marduk, spe[ak for me in my case! May I find justice in your judgement! May the evil of the *induḫallatu*-lizard which fell upon me, (and that of) the *ṣurārû*-lizard which I saw, not approach, not come near, not [press upon (me)], not affect me! May it cross the river! May it pass over the mountain! May it be 3600 miles distant! May it remove from my person! Like smoke may it rise [to heaven]! Like the uprooted tamarisk may it not [return] to its place! May the tamarisk purify me, may the *mashtakal*-plant release me! May earth receive (the evil) from me! May it give forth [its refulgence]! Like the uprooted tamarisk may it not return to its place! Upon it [. . .] may branches sprout forth! The evil of the *induḫallatu*-lizard and of this *ṣurārû*-lizard, may a fish (take it down) to the depths, may a bird take it up to heaven! The evil of the *induḫallatu*-lizard which fell upon me, the portent of evil which I saw–Ea, Shamash and Marduk, turn it to a portent of good, to an oracle of good for me! Undo my guilt! Hear my prayer, at the command of Enlil, king of the gods!

18. – To dissipate the evil of the *induḫallatu* and the *ṣurārû*, you [go to the river] bank. You dig a well. At the edge of the well you draw seven designs with flour. Upon (them) you throw tamarisk, *mashtakal*-plant, date shoots (and) *shalalu*-reed. You have the man kneel over (them). The liturgist[2] stands over him, and three times [that man] raises his eyes. [You recite] the incantation "He angered the god. . . ." You place well water upon his shadow. Into the well you throw (the well water). You sprinkle the water which rises from the . . . over them, seven times toward the right, seven times toward the left. You set out a censer of juniper for Marduk. [You set out] a censer of *pallukku*-plant for [Shamash]. You pour a censer of flour into the river. You recite "Receive, Marduk; receive, Shamash."

Rev. 1'. – . . . to . . . Upon (it) you pour . . . . upon the offering arrangement. To the river . . . . May earth take away the evil . . . . evil to good . . . . You throw . . . into the river, and you swing censer (and) torch [over him. You have him recite as follows].

Rev. 7'. – Incantation: Shamash, great lord of the Igigi and A[nunnaki], director of the black-headed folk, lord of the living and the dead [are you]. Exalted judge whose command cannot [be changed], whose assent no god can alter, you are the lord! Your word is indeed great; your command [is not forgotten]; like (that of) Anu, [your father], your command is supreme; among the gods, your brothers, your word [is pre-eminent].

Noble lord, whose power [is awe-inspiring], merciful god who rules all things! Shamash, as you come forth you see all peoples, you direct the cattle, the beasts of the field(?). Stand by me, Shamash, hear [my] words! Because of the evil of the *ṣurārû*-lizard which [was seen] in my house (and) which confronted me, I, so-and-so, [son of so-and-so], am afraid and frightened. Avert (the evil) [from me], that I may not die, that I may not be wrongly treated! May its evil [not approach me]!

Rev. 23'. – May it cross the river! May it pass over [the mountain]! May it be 3600 miles distant [from my person]! May I, your servant, have health and well-being, that I may [sing] your praise!

Reference. *Or* 34 (1965) 116-120.

Notes. [1]The first line is a philological notation of the scribe indicating that the text from which he was copying was broken at the beginning.

[2]The term "liturgist" (*mušēpišu*) seems to refer to the director of the ritual usually called *mašmāšu*, who is elsewhere addressed directly by the text.

Text 13. Ritual for the evil of evil signs and portents

1. – Namburbi for the evil of evil signs and portents [or a] strange . . . portending scattering of the man's house(hold), [collap] se of the man's house, removal of the man's house, [. . .] of the man's house, revolt or capture of the city: [that its evil] may not approach the man and his house (you perform the following ritual).

6. – You touch [the . . ., fie] lds (and) possessions of the man's estate, as much as there is, and you take up residence(?) in the man's house. You have a stranger, who does not know the man's house, take in his hands a bow, seven arrows with iron heads, seven with copper heads, seven with wooden heads. An iron dagger (and) an axe you bind at his waist. He enters the man's house and takes an arrow and shoots it. He sets aside the bow only, and on the threshold, the gates, the doors (and) the lock of the man's house, with the iron dagger and the axe he makes an incision. Whatever possessions are lying in the courtyard of the man's house, as much as he can carry, you have that man pick up, and you bind his arms behind him. You have him go away (and) cross the river. You spend the night there(?), then you take him to a place he is not familiar with, and the evil will be erased. It will not approach the man and his house.

18. – After this you perform a namburbi against all evil. When you have performed the namburbi, you go to a clay (pile) and "sanctify" the clay. You present a gift to it. You recite three times the incantation "Clay, clay." You take clay[1] and you make a substitution-image. You dress it in a woolen garment. You make a likeness of the portent. You scrape off the thresholds (and) the doors with a lead axe, and you sweep the rooms, the courtyards (and) the beams with a datepalm branch, and you convey the refuse to the river. Then you take out the substitution-image (and) the likeness of the portent that you made, along with the refuse, to the river, and at the river bank you sweep the ground (and) sprinkle pure water. You set up a reed altar before Shamash. You offer sacrifices.[2] You set out an offering arrangement. . . . You put the substitution-image, together with the likeness of the portent, before the offering arrangement, facing Shamash. Before Shamash [you recite] as follows.

26. – Incantation: Shamash, [you indeed] are king of heaven and earth, judge of the upper and lower regions, light of the gods, governor of mankind, the one who renders judgement over the great gods. I have turned to you, I have sought you out among (all) the gods. Command (my) health! Because of the evil of evil signs (and) portents which have repeatedly taken place against me, I am afraid, I am terrified, I am in dread. Avert this portent from me, that I may not die, that I may not be wronged, that I may sing your praise!

31. – When you have recited this you go away (to stand) over the image and you recite as follows.[3]

32. – [Incantation]: I have given you [as my ex]change(?), I have given you as my ransom, [I have given you] as my substitute. I have stripped off all the evil of my body onto you, I have stripped off all the evil of my flesh [onto you, I have stripped off all the evil] of my sinews onto you, I have stripped off all the evil beside me, I have stripped off all the evil at my right and my left [onto you(?), I have stripped off all the evil] before me and behind me onto you.

36. – When you have recited this, you depart from before Shamash and recite as follows to the river.[4]

37. – [Incantation]: You, River, are creator of all things. I, so-and-so, son of so-and-so, whose god is so-and-so, whose goddess is so-and-so, because evil signs (and) portents have repeatedly taken place against me, am terrified, afraid, and in dread. Just as this image and likeness of the portent do not return to their place, may the evil of those things[5] not approach, may it not come near, may it not press, may it not affect me! May the evil of those things not return to its place, may the evil of those things be far from my person! May the evil of those things be erased from my person, may the evil of those things be dissipated from my person! That the evil of those things may not approach my person, that the evil of those things may not come near my person, that the evil of those things may not press upon my person, may the evil of those things rise like smoke to heaven, may the evil of those things, like the uprooted tamarisk, not return to its place, that I may daily bless you, River, that those who see me may forever sing your praise! Take that evil away! Take it down to your depths!

48. – When you have recited this, you throw the image and likeness of that portent into the river. The sweepings of the house, the datepalm broom, the scrapings that you have scraped from the thresholds and gates, (and) the refuse you convey (away), and place them on a boat going downstream. You put that man who commissioned the ritual with his garment fringe into the river. Then he immerses himself three times facing upstream, three times facing downstream, and he recites as follows.

53. – You, River, take away from my person that evil which was placed upon me! May an alternate (woman) serve as substitute for me, may a replacement receive it from me, may a surrogate[6] receive it from me! May the day bring me health, the month gladness, the year abundance! Ea, Shamash and Marduk, help me! May the evil signs (and) portents which were placed upon me be dissolved!

58. – When he has recited this, you lead him up from the river, and he removes his garment and washes with tamarisk sap. He is fumigated with cedar, juniper and sulphur. He recites seven times "Ea performed (the incantation), Ea undid (the evil)," and without looking behind him he enters a different house and spends the night (there). He approaches[7] a foreign (or: strange) woman. In the morning he sends that woman out, and a man lays hold on the sins of that man(?), then you gather (them) into (a piece of) clay, and that man recites as follows.

64. – I have removed my evils, I have stripped off my sins. May this day receive from me the evil of the signs (and) portents which have been placed on me and send (it) across the river! Ninmah, who created god and man, has given me judgement.

67. – When he has recited this, he throws the evil of those things into the river. He sprinkles water from a holy-water container over the bed and the bedspread(?). He recites "Ea performed (the incantation), Ea undid (the evil)," and he leaves his house, without taking the road he took (in coming). He goes to another place. [For three days] he does not enter his house. On the fourth[8] day he enters his house. Its evil will be dissipated. That man will stand victorious over his opponent-at-law.[9]

Colophon (Exemplar A). – Finished. Written [accor]ding to a (wooden) tablet; not collated. [Tablet of] Sîn-šar-ilāni, the apprentice, the young incantation priest.

Colophon (Exemplar B). – [Namburbi] for evil, untoward portents. Written [according to] its original (and) col[lated]. (Illegible traces follow.)

References. *Or* 39 (1970) 142-151; *Or* 40 (1971) 182; *Or* 43 (1974) in press.

Notes. [1]"Clay" here translates *ṭidu*; in the preceding lines it translates *kullatu*.

[2]The logogram used suggests animal sacrifices.

[3]Line numbering from here on follows BM 59808; this text has no divider before or after line 31.

[4]Though the direction to depart "from before Shamash" is found in both copies, we expect "from the image."

[5]In this and the following sentences, BM 59808 substitutes "the evil of the same" (ḪUL MIN) for "the evil of those things"; both refer to the image and the likeness of the portent, which now bear the evil.

[6]BM 59808: "surrogates."

[7]The verb implies sexual "approaching."

[8]"Fourth" is from BM 59808; K.2777+ has "on the third day."

[9]This sentence is a standard omen apodosis predicting success.

Text 14. Ritual to secure brisk trade[1]

1. – That brisk trade may [not] bypass (lit. forget) the house of a tavernkeeper, or diviner, or physician, or liturgist, or baker. Its ritual: you crush dust from a temple, dust from a god's dais, dust from a city gate, dust from a ditch, dust from an open air shrine, dust from a bridge on which Ishtar[2] shines, dust from a crossroads, dust from a dust storm, dust from a prostitute's door, dust from the door of a . . ., dust from a weaver's door, dust from a palace door, dust from a malt-grower's door, dust from a tavernkeeper's door, dust from a road, dust from a gardener's door, dust from a carpenter's door, dust from the door of a *nadītu*-priestess, all these kinds of dust. You mix them together in river water. You smear cypress oil on them. With the paste you anoint the door of the man's house. You sweep the roof. You sprinkle pure water. You set up a reed altar before Ishtar. You arrange twelve loaves. You set out confections of honey and ghee. You scatter dates and fine flour. You set out a censer of juniper. You bring (the afflicted person), whether male or female, up to the roof. You have him kneel down and you set a copper image to (his) right. He recites as follows: "Ishtar, Nanay, and Gazbaya[3] help me in this matter!" He recites this, and recounts the matters which are on his mind. Then there will always be brisk trade for the tavern. That house will be prosperous in the future.

21. – Incantation: Ishtar, most courageous of the great gods, exalted, glorious, warlike Ishtar, noble one, most great lady Irnini, help me! You are (by turns) fair and darkened.[4] Lady-Enlil of (all) people, goddess of males, outdoer of (all) people, mighty[5] Ishtar, daughter of Anu, created by the great gods, giver of the scepter, the throne (and) the royal staff to all kings, lady of (all) lands, heed me! Proudest of goddesses, exalted lady, I call upon you: help me! May the censer rich(ly laden) with pure juniper come before you! Ishtar, stand by me to (further) my affairs! May this tavern trade be your tavern trade! Ishtar, lay your hand on the potstand and mixing vat! May profit come my way, and never cease! You are the one who has this office. End-formula of the incantation.

38. – The spell "If profit is cut off from the house of a tavernkeeper."

39. – Its ritual: you place a censer of juniper before Ishtar, and libate the tavernkeeper's beer. Do not finish (the libation, but) save (some of the beer), then you prostrate yourself and libate the beer (that remains). Then there will always be brisk trade for the tavern. It will be prosperous in the future.

43. – Incantation: Ishtar of the lands, most heroic of goddesses, this is your priestly residence: exult and rejoice! Come, enter our house! With you may your sweet bedfellow enter, your lover and your cult-actor! May my lips be honey, my hands charm! May the lip(s) of my vulva(?) be lip(s) of honey! As the birds twitter over a snake which comes out of its hole, may these people fight over me! From the priestly residence of Ishtar, from the temple residence of Ninlil, from among the possessions of Ningizzida, seize ye him, bring him here, be gracious to him! May the distant one return to me, may the angry one come back to me! Like smoke[6] may his heart return to me! As the rain fructifies the earth, so that vegetation is abundant, may the greetings addressed to me be abundant! End-formula of the incantation.[7]

60. – The spell "Brisk trade for the innkeeper on the quai."

61. – Its ritual: dust from a quai, dust from a crossing, dust from a bridge, dust from an intersection of four roads, dust from a crossroads, dust from a city gate, dust from a dais, dust from the door of the Ishtar temple,

dust from a prostitute's house, dust from the door of a tavernkeeper's house where trade is plentiful–(you take) all these dusts. Before Ishtar you set up a reed altar. You set out three offerings of breast(-shaped) bread. You set out a censer of juniper. You libate fine beer. You recite the incantation seven times and prostrate yourself. You mix those dusts with water. You recite the incantation seven times (again) and (with the mixture) you wash the door of the house, and with what remains of it you make an im[age of] an ox and bury it under a vat.

Colophon (Exemplar A). – (Catchline:) If a man's seal is broken or lost or [dropped] in a river. Tablet 135 of the nambu[rbis]. (Twelve-line Aššurbanipal ownership formula follows).

Colophon (Exemplar B). – Written according to an original tablet of Babylon. Hastily (!) excerpted.

References. *ABRT* I 66f. + Lenormant, *Choix* 99; *KAR* 144.

Notes. [1]This text has been most recently treated by Ebeling, *RA* 49 (1955) 178-184. Internal titles divide this tablet into three sections, each giving a ritual for a similar purpose. The titles of lines 38 and 60 have the formula INIM(or KA).INIM.MA, here translated "spell"; this formula is normally used in a final subscript to identify the preceding text, but in the present instance it is clearly a text *heading* to which the following ritual directions refer. For another instance of internal division, see text 7, note 1.

[2]The goddess is here identified with the Venus star.

[3]The last two names are here alternate names for *ᵈIš-tar* with the verb in the singular.

[4]This is a further astral reference.

[5]On *telītu* see J. Nougayrol, *RA* 62 (1968) 94.

[6]KÚ.GI = *qu₅-tāri*. This image is: as smoke rises willy-nilly, so may his affections turn compulsively to me.

[7]This incantation, following on the title "If profit is cut off from the house of a tavernkeeper," suggests a relation between tavernkeeping and prostitution.